What teachers
need to know about
Social and
emotional
development

What teachers
need to know about

What teachers need to know about Social and emotional development

ROS LEYDEN
AND ERIN SHALE

ACER Press

KH

First published 2012
by ACER Press, an imprint of
Australian Council *for* Educational Research Ltd
19 Prospect Hill Road, Camberwell
Victoria, 3124, Australia

www.acerpress.com.au
sales@acer.edu.au

Edited by Holly Proctor
Cover design, text design and typesetting by ACER Project Publishing
Printed in Australia by BPA Print Group

National Library of Australia Cataloguing-in-Publication entry

Author:	Leyden, Ros.
Title:	What teachers need to know about social and emotional development / Ros Leyden; Erin Shale.
ISBN:	9781742860336 (pbk.)
Notes:	Includes bibliographical references and index.
Subjects:	Social interaction in children.
	Social skills in children.
	Emotions in children.
Other Authors/Contributors:	
	Shale, Erin.
Dewey Number:	303.32

10/20/14

Foreword

The social and emotional development of children is now a central concern in both primary and secondary schools around the world. For children to succeed in a multicultural, emotionally demanding, economically changing and target-driven culture they must have access to learning about a whole range of skills that will be important for their future lives. Difficult behaviour significantly impacts on learning and children cannot thrive academically unless they are emotionally stable. As recent government initiatives in the UK and Australia demonstrate, this will only be achieved when the major focus is the holistic development of learners rather than just the testing, gathering of statistics and the narrow view of academic success and school accountability.

With personal and social development at the core of the curriculum, it is hoped that children and young people will learn to 'read' their emotions, be able to make successful friendships, and confidently meet new challenges and new situations. Teachers, however, face enormous challenges in meeting the emotional and academic needs of their learners. In this book, Ros Leyden and Erin Shale provide an interrogative framework for the promotion of children's social and emotional development. Recognising that there is no one magic recipe to follow they discuss and present readers with a range of approaches that can be adjusted to differing school contexts. This will generate dialogue amongst teachers who understand that being effective in the classroom requires the space and opportunity to deal with problems in children's lives more effectively, and a curriculum that supports their personal needs as well as their academic ones. This holistic, 'inside-out' development of children takes them and their teachers on a journey of discovery that makes all of us more reflective and affords children the respect and regard they deserve.

Rosalyn George
Professor of Education and Equality, University of London

Contents

Preface

School, and the people at school, form a significant part of a child's world. Children who are unhappy at school have a diminished childhood and carry negative images through life that can have lasting effects on their social and emotional development. School should set children up for life and give them the skills and opportunities to develop to their full potential. Every child is unique and the work teachers undertake can be life altering for children. More than ever, teachers need great knowledge and insight into the complex environment in which children live and the impact this has on their social and emotional development. Mental illness is the largest cause of non-fatal disability in Australia with most adult mental illnesses having their onset in childhood. An astounding 14 per cent of children and young people have a mental disorder (Department of Health and Ageing, 2010). Children who do not have mental health issues may still experience some social and emotional dysfunction or other setbacks in these important formative years. Clearly, teachers should be able to identify children requiring special support and have the strategies to enhance the social and emotional growth of every child. While parenting is the most important job in the world, this book should equip teachers to tackle more confidently what is arguably the second most important job: teaching.

The major focus of this book is to provide busy teachers with knowledge and insights into the social and emotional development of children. These insights are underpinned by the latest Australian and international research conducted by highly respected educationalists, psychologists and experts in the field of child development. We also strive to empower teachers by offering practical strategies to lighten their workload, not increase it. Some strategies may be memory joggers, while others will provide new approaches to consider. These cover behaviour management, classroom activities and posters and newsletter items to encourage parental involvement in children's social and emotional development. We also highlight the key signs that indicate children may be suffering from depression, eating disorders, anxiety and other serious issues. Early intervention can prevent children from unnecessary distress and help them regain their emotional footing as quickly as possible.

To say that teachers are also social workers, mentors, 'parents', emotional coaches and significant others is simply telling it like it is. Yet, despite the amazing work they do, teachers are sometimes reluctant to seek reassurance and support when facing difficult children or classes, fearing they may be seen as incapable of handling challenging situations. Teaching can be a complex and lonely business. Armed with an understanding of how children develop socially and emotionally, however, teachers can more confidently support children in the classroom and discern when there is a need to seek advice from leadership or colleagues before organising referrals to outside health professionals.

The book can be read in its entirety to gain a sound understanding of the social and emotional development of children or information on specific issues can be 'cherry picked'. Underpinned by the latest research, strategies and insights in this book will lighten teachers' emotional workload and allow them to channel more energy into teaching and enjoying their vital contribution to the formation of happy and resilient young people.

PART ONE

5 to 12
– The big picture

What's happening? Ages, stages and milestones

The importance of social and emotional health

Children all start school with different expectations, hopes and even fears. Some are socially competent, eager to learn and bursting with confidence. Others stand back in the shadows, plagued with insecurities and lacking basic survival skills for this new and demanding world. Educators worldwide are far more concerned about young children's social-emotional and behavioural deficits than their delays in cognitive skills (Whitted, 2011). When children's thoughts are dominated by worries, they can be completely 'absent' in the classroom. Children with high social and emotional intelligence are well-equipped to be happy, successful and handle the ups and downs of life. Conversely, children lacking important social and emotional skills can have difficulty forming positive relationships, which leads to increasing frustration, withdrawal or negative behaviour. These children can enter a downward spiral of unhappiness, school failure and even expulsion. All teachers, parents and those interested in our children's wellbeing must understand these long-term implications; but above all, they must know how to change this situation.

Emotions affect how children think and act, what they attempt or avoid and their ability to socialise with others. Children who are socially and emotionally competent are also more resilient and do better academically (Cadima et al., 2010; Malecki & Elliott, 2002). Time spent teaching children to identify and manage feelings is time well spent. Emotions shape teaching and learning. Great teachers are skilled social and emotional detectives. With high emotional intelligence, they keenly observe children's behaviour, identifying those who are off-track developmentally or captives of difficult emotions. As Schutz and DeCuir (2002) conclude, teachers' ability to 'read' students' frustration, anxiety and other emotions is the first step in helping children recognise and manage them.

Emotional intelligence (EI) was popularised by Daniel Goleman's best-selling book *Emotional intelligence: Why it can matter more than IQ* (1996). Emotional intelligence is now universally recognised as a key to success in all aspects of life: making and maintaining friends; relating positively to others; maintaining good mental and physical health; maximising academic performance; and remaining resilient despite setbacks. In essence, being emotionally intelligent leads to a richer and more fulfilling life.

What do you remember most from your own school days? Most people we have spoken to remember people, friendships and fights far more than specific curriculum or results. Even for adults, fitting in socially, being liked and accepted is high on most wish lists. For children, they are make-or-break. A dramatic increase in the complexity of their social world confronts children as they move from preschool to primary school. Those unable to mix socially with others, or unable to manage and express emotions appropriately, are soon left behind. Moving through middle childhood, the peer group increases in importance. These years are a training ground for adolescence where avoiding embarrassment and, above all, finding acceptance from peers are the cornerstones of a young person's happiness. Although identity formation is one of the most important tasks of adolescence, children aged 5 and 6 have already started making sense of who they are, as they seek to fit in and proudly show their achievements. Children with excellent social and emotional skills have a stronger foundation upon which to complete identity formation and make safer decisions as they step onto that infamous roller-coaster called 'adolescence'.

The great news is that social and emotional skills can be taught to all children, from the most charming and cooperative to those who 'bless' teachers with sleepless nights. The acquisition of social and emotional skills must not be an 'add-on' in the curriculum, but given the highest priority. These skills free children to thrive and enjoy what should be some of the happiest and most carefree days of their young lives. Although these skills should be modelled by teachers and taught explicitly and sequentially through discreet lessons, they should also be reinforced every day in the same way as academic skills, forming an integral part of the school curriculum (Fenty et al., 2008). However, teachers must first be able to assess the current state of each child's social and emotional world. What are the obstacles facing this child at home and at school? What is preventing this child from coming into the classroom worry-free and ready to learn? All teachers experience those nagging suspicions that something, or someone, is preventing particular students from making the most of school. There are many common underlying issues for teachers to consider when they notice that something is not quite right with a child. Questions to ask when evaluating a child's social and emotional health include:

- How well do I know this child's home situation? Are parents physically and emotionally well? Are relationships within the home harmonious? Is this family experiencing any significant stress?
- Why is this child always late, disorganised, tired, unable to concentrate, moody or lacking in self-control? Can previous teachers offer any insights?
- Has this child recently lost a close friend or has there been a friendship rift?
- Are there signs of bullying, depression, an eating disorder or other serious issues? (See Chapters 10 and 11.)
- Has behaviour changed significantly? Is the child more withdrawn, angry, moody, tired, demanding or attention seeking? (See Chapter 6.)
- Have academic results suddenly declined?
- Does this child have breakfast and an adequate lunch?
- Is this child's school uniform clean? Are there hygiene issues? (See Chapter 7.)
- Is this child anxious about tests or other forms of assessment? Do the parents have unrealistically high expectations?
- Can the child tell you more? Initiate conversations with children who appear unsettled. If drawings or written work reflect unhappiness, gently weave this into conversations: 'Jason, I noticed that you were very quiet last week. Is everything all right?' Many children are immensely relieved to have a caring adult with whom to share sad family events or a fight with a special friend.
- Should you be in touch with parents? Rather than waiting until formal parent-teacher meetings, initiate conversations that can often uncover issues affecting children. Start conversations positively by praising children's efforts or achievements before broaching concerns.

An overview of social and emotional development

Although all children do not follow exactly the same developmental trajectory, there are common patterns. Child psychologist Erik Erikson (1963) developed the time-honoured theory of psychosocial development from birth to old age. He described various stages during which conflicts (challenges) act as positive or negative turning points in development (see Chapter 4). Resolving challenges successfully promotes personal growth, while failures delay growth and result in negative effects. Erikson's theory contains many important messages for today's teachers. Children from ages 5 to 12 navigate an enormously important period of their lives. Whether they come from warm and loving families or fractured and disadvantaged homes, all must strengthen their existing social and emotional skills to face developmental challenges and successfully resolve inevitable conflicts.

While every child is unique, there is a set of ideal skills, milestones and behaviours to expect at each stage of their social and emotional development. Some children arrive at school bursting with confidence and excitement, armed with a kitbag of skills. Others arrive ill-prepared. For them, school is a scary place. Despite the unlevel playing fields of life, every child faces the same social and emotional challenges. Teachers can make the world of difference to a child's ability to tackle challenges well. The set of tables on the following pages provide a snapshot of the expected social and emotional development of children from ages 5 to 12. It includes the major milestones and issues facing children at each age; their greatest fears, hopes, needs and aspirations. Remembering that children develop at their own unique pace, having a general idea of what to expect helps teachers provide the best possible support for children in their care.

Snapshot of children's social and emotional development from ages 5 to 6

What's happening from ages 5 to 6? (Foundation Year or first year of school)

Starting school is a major transition for children. It signals the move from infancy and play to more structured, formal learning and higher expectations. These children need sound social and emotional skills to thrive in this new and complex environment. It is an exciting, but anxious, time of change: a year of massive growth, exploration and uncertainty about the world.

What do children aged 5 to 6 look like? (Free range chickens ... active, energetic and not yet in control. Generally happy and a joy to see!)

At this age they:

- want to fit in and are eager to cooperate
- observe adults and copy behaviour
- desire approval – 'Look at me!'
- have fewer uncontrolled outbursts of emotion
- are beginning to manage impulses and to control their desire for instant gratification
- generally agree to rules but don't like losing
- are still egocentric but capable of feeling and expressing empathy
- have a concept of right and wrong that is emerging
- need the security of clear boundaries, guidance and structures consistently reinforced
- enjoy telling jokes
- enjoy the opportunity to do jobs (boosts self-esteem)
- are developing a sense of pride in accomplishments
- still need nurturing and adult reassurance but want to 'grow up' and taste some independence.

Social tasks are to:

- develop greater empathy
- establish and maintain positive relationships/friendships
- start developing a sense of morality
- control impulsive behaviour.

Emotional tasks are to:

- identify and manage emotions
- form a positive self-concept and self-esteem (identity formation has begun)
- become resilient
- begin to function more independently (from looking after personal possessions to making decisions without needing constant support).

Red alerts:

- Despite growing understanding of right and wrong, children of this age can often fib, cheat or take belongings of others.
- Teasing about difference begins at this age.
- Children as young as 3 can experience bullying.
- Children as young as 3 can suffer from depression.
- Children as young as 5 can develop eating disorders.
- The desire to be autonomous needs nurturing – integral to self-confidence.

Snapshot of children's social and emotional development from ages 6 to 7

What's happening from ages 6 to 7? (Years 1 and 2)

Children at this age are feeling more settled and comfortable at school. They have a more confident swagger although their identity is still fluid and a work of art in progress. This is a time of great discovery and the world is like an adventure park for them. A social order is emerging within their peer group.

What do children aged 6 to 7 look like? (Pecking order becoming evident.)

At this age they:

- generally enjoy school
- take life and responsibility more seriously
- want to be the 'best' and 'first'
- are letting go of fantasy ... more grounded in reality
- are anxious to please and need approval, reassurance and praise
- want to do everything well
- need acceptance from peers, teachers and family
- experience friendship mayhem – best friends one minute, enemies the next
- have their feelings easily hurt – confidence can be paper thin
- love jokes – 'Knock, knock'
- are beginning to discover that parents do not know everything (thankfully, many still believe teachers can walk on water)
- may swear more often to test adults' reactions
- can be oppositional, silly and critical ('It's her fault ... It's not fair')
- find being corrected and losing at games difficult and may sulk, cry, refuse to play or reinvent rules to suit themselves
- are easily disappointed and frustrated by self-perceived failure. They still need nurturing and help in developing positive self-talk and confidence
- can discuss more complex moral issues.

Social tasks are to:

- form opinions about moral values – right and wrong
- be able to express an opinion and negotiate
- develop greater empathy
- begin understanding different viewpoints.

Emotional tasks are to:

- start making more sense of who I am ('Who am I like? Who likes me?')
- develop a sense of family history (identity)
- grapple with questions about death
- accept that parents are not all-powerful (but teachers are!).

Red Alerts:

- Some girls as young as 6 years old exhibit body dissatisfaction.
- Girls with higher weight status believe they are less intelligent and have lower self-esteem.
- Children who have not yet formed friendships could be at risk and need support.

- Comparison with others escalates at this age and can lead to more bullying.
- Many children this age worry about parents being vulnerable, separating and even dying.

Snapshot of children's social and emotional development from ages 8 to 9

What's happening from ages 8 to 9? (Years 3 and 4)

This is the time when TWEENS emerge and children are demanding greater independence and desperately want to be seen as 'grown up'. This is an exciting but scary time of transition. They are beginning to ponder some huge questions as part of forming their identity while rushing into these pre-pubescent years. The major questions they dwell on are: 'Am I normal? Does everyone feel like this? Should my body look like this? Why do I have these feelings?'

What do children aged 8 to 9 look like? (Burning desire to fly solo.)

At this age:

- they are thoughtful, mature and sophisticated one minute, irresponsible and impulsive the next (Some 8-year-olds may still believe in Father Christmas.)
- many adopt a know-it-all attitude and become argumentative with peers and teachers ('You said we could …')
- they still desire attention and recognition from teachers
- they experience a time of great intellectual development and the ability to think abstractly and be more critical (Tweens are hit with the awful realisation that adults – parents *and teachers* – are not always right!)
- belonging and acceptance by peers is important – they enjoy team games and activities
- most have one 'best friend'
- secrets and loyalty to friends rule the day.

Social tasks are to:

- fit in and be accepted by peers (preoccupied with comparisons – 'Do I fit in?')
- have a 'best friend'
- strengthen cooperative skills.

Red Alerts:

- Some girls as young as 8 years old reach puberty – some sail through first menstruation, while others are quite fragile. This can be particularly frightening for ill-prepared children.
- Early and late physical developers can face anxiety and possible teasing.

Emotional tasks are to:

- adjust to a sexually developing body and handle the agonies of feeling awkward and self-conscious ('What will I look like? Do I look normal?')
- continue refining a sense of self (fluid and constantly changing)
- work out values and beliefs – often passionately adopt an ethical stance ('I'm a vegetarian. I'm joining Save the Bears.')
- establish independence and individuality (intensely private; wanting alone-time; displays of non-compliance at school and home).

- Some children, particularly girls, are overwhelmed with physical and emotional changes and can become moody, distracted or withdrawn.
- Pressure to 'keep up' is starting earlier and earlier (this applies to both boys and girls) and is exacerbated by media images of the 'perfect' body and the latest fashion and fads.

Snapshot of children's social and emotional development from ages 10 to 11

What's happening from ages 10 to 11? (Years 5 and 6)

Children at this age are facing one of the biggest transitions in childhood; from primary to secondary school. Some children can't wait while others are anxious and frightened, although wild horses couldn't drag this admission from them. These are the years of paradox; children display leadership, maturity and a sense of fun as well as restlessness, moodiness and silliness.

What do children aged 10 to 11 look like? (Turbulence affects the flight path – the infamous roller-coaster years begin.)

At this age:

- they are a big fish in a little pond – they act outwardly cool and feisty
- they are inwardly – confused – uncertainty and turmoil rule
- 'best friend blues' wound deeply – they can be broken-hearted when friendships collapse
- even loyal friendships can be volatile – especially for girls
- acceptance by peers is paramount
- they are competitive and want to excel
- boys still enjoy rough-and-tumble
- they have a strong sense of justice. It is a period of moral development
- rules are harder to enforce due to the desire to impress peers rather than adults – and adults aren't always right anyway!
- they have a growing awareness of gender differences and sexuality
- they need reassurance about secondary school and opportunities to discuss concerns and have questions answered.

Social tasks are to:

- behave appropriately in a variety of social situations
- refine communication skills
- resolve interpersonal conflicts – understand the difference between passive, assertive and aggressive responses
- become more independent and responsible for actions
- value and respect rules and authority
- know how to act appropriately and safely in the cyber social world.

Emotional tasks are to:

- manage emotional changes accompanying puberty (torn between needing the security of the familiar and craving the unknown)
- develop more positive self-esteem and resilience by building strengths and accepting limitations
- acknowledge 'who I am' through an optimistic lens.

Red Alerts:

- Girls and boys need well-developed emotional skills to ride the ups and downs of hormonal waves.
- The bullying of others increases as children get older – 10 years and upwards.
- Not until the age of 10 will most children fully understand the finality of death – sensitive support is needed at times of bereavement.
- At this age some children may be floundering and anxious about stepping up and facing secondary school expectations.

Snapshot of children's social and emotional development from age 12 and onwards

What's happening from age 12 and onwards? (Year 7)

Children at this age are on the cliff edge of the teenage years. They are facing a huge transition into secondary school, which can be as scary as, or even more so than, the transition into primary school. This is when they need to call upon the crucial social and emotional skills they have been developing in the primary years. Now, they are the small fish in the big pond. They need to develop new social networks to affirm them and support their ongoing identity formation. The burning questions they grapple with are: 'Who am I?' (this is central to the formation of identity); and 'Am I normal?' (a question that can take years to answer).

What do children aged 12 look like? (Torn between the desperate desire to be part of the flock and wanting to be seen as an individual.)

At this age:

- confusion still reigns supreme – how should a teenager behave? What kind of teenager will I be?
- it is a time of loss – the familiar (childhood) is rapidly disappearing and the future (teenage years) is uncertain
- they need to feel normal and fit in with peers
- they are anxious to look in control and avoid embarrassment at all costs – worry about appearance
- it is a time of flexing muscles and trying on various 'masks' as part of identity formation – testing and pushing boundaries

- they continue to crave privacy and independence
- peers rule – fitting in and being accepted is more important than anything else – including academic results, parents, siblings, the family dog … and teachers
- friends know better and more than any adult ever could
- they are sensitive and easily hurt
- often they will not comply readily – they need reasons why.

Social tasks are to:

- establish independence
- adjust to a bigger social world with greater expectations and demands
- overcome the awkward and clumsy stage
- find acceptance within a peer group
- become more self-assured and able to say 'No!'

Emotional tasks are to:

- move further away from family and closer to friends for support
- handle issues and growing concerns about sexuality and relationships
- manage confusing and unexpected feelings, such as anger and rebellion
- move towards self-acceptance.

Red Alerts:

- 'Big fish to little fish' syndrome can find some children experiencing a dip in self-esteem as they enter secondary school.
- Increasing pressure on children to grow up and be sophisticated can cause anxiety.
- Exposure to social networking and the media can confuse and worry some children as they question themselves and where they sit in the world. Watch out for risk-taking, anxiety and depression.

- Raging hormones can cause moodiness, headaches, aches and pains and sleep problems in some children.
- There is a huge variation in physical and emotional development between girls and boys – from 12 to 14 is the growth spurt period for most boys. Late developing boys may stand out from peers and suffer from a lack of self-esteem.

gress res...
ation practice
ics foundation se...

personal we...
...pathy individual progress
...eing values co...ic...ion pr

t w o

The new world of childhood

Being a child today

The childhood remembered by teachers and parents is dramatically different to that experienced by today's child. Childhood today is undeniably faster and more socially and emotionally demanding. In this complex real world, these 'too-much-too-fast-too-soon' kids must also navigate the virtual world with its many allures and dangers. Children today speak a language parents and teachers often struggle to decipher. Priceless childhood innocence can be lost in the blink of an eye or, more accurately, computer screen. It is common to see preschoolers as young as 15 months entertaining themselves with their parents' smartphone or tablet computer, competently sweeping through the screens to find their favourite app. Most children in Years 5 and 6 have access to prepaid phones, often with the explanation that these are for safety reasons. Children live with multiple televisions and computers at home, with many having both in their bedrooms. Gaming is growing in popularity with more girls entering what was once chiefly the domain of boys. Facebook's terms of service require users to be at least 13 years old, yet children as young as 10 openly admit to being on Facebook, often with their parents' consent. Although highly skilled with technology, many children lack the maturity to understand the nuances and potential dangers social media presents. Cyberbullying is escalating and well-publicised cases highlight its potentially tragic outcomes. Teachers and parents must also strive to protect children from overexposure to often sensationalised media images and issues children are emotionally unable to process. Too much information, too early, can confuse children and impede healthy social and emotional development. Children who 'grow up' too early can develop stress-related health issues, such as headaches, nervousness, hyperactivity and eating disorders (Doherty, 2000).

Modern-day technologies and social networking sites are contributing significantly to child and adolescent anxiety and a growing number of children need therapy to handle associated distress. This is due to the ability to be in contact 24/7. In previous generations, you had the telephone and, if you were lucky, mum and dad let you make a call after you got home from school. But now, primary school children, not to mention adolescents, have mobiles and internet access, which means they are constantly in touch via text messages and Facebook. Children are using networking sites to determine their identity and form a view of what society thinks of them and this, sadly, is not always a positive view.

DARRYL CROSS, PSYCHOLOGIST

Identity formation begins right from the early years when children gradually begin making sense of who they are and it becomes the most important task of adolescence. When children use internet sites, rather than their peers, as a reference point for identity formation, they are at increased risk of becoming confused and overly self-critical in their desperate bid to fit into the adult world.

To grow, we must be risk 'literate'. In the artificial world of computer technology, realistic video games and social networking, children's lives are increasingly devoid of authentic experiences that teach effective risk-taking. This is a serious problem for healthy psychological development. Children need to test their competencies in the real world with real-world consequences.

SIMON CRISP, PSYCHOLOGIST

Teachers give children authentic experiences by ensuring they have teamwork opportunities where they must relate to others in real-time and develop vital interpersonal skills. However, while keeping children connected to the real world, teachers must acknowledge the positive aspects of technology, which can be a powerful tool to engage students in their learning while developing essential social and emotional skills.

I decided to incorporate 'home' technologies into classroom learning experiences after hearing one student say that staying home was more fun because he could play on his Nintendo DS® and Wii™. My class and I discovered that games-based learning is often nonlinear, fast paced, rewarding, compelling and fun.

Gaming and other technologies are wholly integrated into our curriculum and are a vehicle for powerful learning. We use Lure of the Labyrinth, a free online mathematics game, to explore mathematical concepts before any explicit teaching occurs. This encourages students to learn by doing, to notice patterns and cause and effect within a puzzle, to ask questions of each other and their families and to make links to content when explicit teaching begins. We use Nintendo DS®, Wii™, PlayStation®2 and the iPod Touch® in reading groups. Students experience the game, complete an activity related to the game (for example, measuring heart rates before and after playing tennis on Wii™Sports and investigating why their heart rates differ), reflect on what they have learned and share it with the grade. My students know there is a learning goal linked to using gaming, and have become adept at identifying their learning. Games promote the development of 21st century skills such as communication, collaboration, critical thinking, creativity and problem solving.

The use of gaming has rekindled a love of learning in many of my students – some who perhaps had not enjoyed school for some time. Gaming has changed their idea of what learning looks like, feels like and sounds like, and has opened them to new approaches to learning, such as collaboration and exploration. Parent perception of technology in the classroom has changed. If children love coming to school, parents will support what we do in the classroom. As educators we must think outside the square and ensure the world within our classrooms keeps up with the world of our students. Great teachers use great tools and, increasingly, gaming is becoming one of them.

LYNETTE BARR, PRIMARY TEACHER

Despite the advantages technology brings, many children are spending too much time online, some up to 8 or 10 hours a week (Watson, 2010). Researchers are concerned that excessive exposure to internet stimulus could be altering the very architecture of children's brains due to the stress of constant alertness. There has been a 300 per cent rise in prescriptions of Ritalin® over the last decade and many children who demand instant gratification and constant entertainment are losing the ability to entertain themselves and spend time in quiet thought (Watson, 2010).

The increased sexualisation of young children, particularly girls, is another frightening example of too much, too soon (Doherty, 2000). Merchandise such as padded bras for 7-year-olds brings undue pressure to grow up fast. Magazines targeted at children also pressure young girls to mirror the slinky model look and boys to develop a 'sixpack'. Not surprisingly, an increasing number of children are developing eating disorders at disturbingly young ages (see Chapter 11).

> *Childhood is being eroded as kids are pressured to grow up too early. Children in primary school are already worrying about their appearance, having the right look, the right clothes. This pressure on children potentially impacts on their confidence and self-esteem and implies that self-worth is related to attractiveness and image. Media and advertising reinforce gender stereotypes with a negative impact on development. Depression, social anxiety and eating disorders may result.*
>
> **LOUISE NEWMAN, AM, PROFESSOR OF DEVELOPMENTAL PSYCHIATRY, MONASH UNIVERSITY**

Paradoxically, while children today have enormous 'freedom' through access to the media and sophisticated technology, few enjoy the unsupervised freedoms cherished by previous generations who played cricket barefoot in the street or played happily in local parks. Children learn through mistakes, scrapes, fights and falls, not through sterilised environments. A world that is too safe can delay cognitive, social and emotional development. It prevents children from developing a reservoir of experiences to draw upon when handling future hurdles and disappointments. Parents who see the world as unsafe and dangerous zealously eliminate even healthy risk-taking. Most believe that crime is increasing and worry their children will become victims. Although statistics reveal crime rates are not increasing (Sutterby, 2009; Zubrick et al., 2010), almost 90 per cent of parents believe it is unsafe for children to catch public transport alone and 73 per cent see 'stranger danger' as an impediment to children playing in public spaces (VicHealth, 2011). Alarmingly, three-quarters of parents drive their children to school, even over short distances. Independent travel gives children increased social interactions with other children while increasing self-esteem, independence and confidence. Parental fears are easily communicated to children, preventing them from testing and expanding their social and emotional wings. It is significant that children report noticing the absence of other children playing on their street and worry about traffic and stranger danger (Garrard, 2009). Developing a sense of trust and safety in their world is a basic need in early childhood (Erikson, 1963). Caring and empathetic teachers can develop children's sense of personal safety, at least while in their school world, despite parental angst, media-generated alarm and in-your-face images invading every home.

Today's over-protected children are also frequently over-scheduled. Well-intentioned parents manically strive to be good parents by 'enriching' their children's lives; most afternoons involve music lessons, swimming, drama or similar. Pressure is also increasing on ever younger children to compete academically as many parents push their children to get ahead and stay ahead of the pack through tutoring from commercial companies. Growing up should be a time of developmentally-appropriate discovery and unfolding wonder, not a competition or a race. While extension activities and even tutoring can be beneficial, we must guard against these taking over children's lives. Children need time to be children. Some thrive in a hyper-busy, pressure-cooker environment, but others suffer stress, anxiety and even depression (Elkind, 2001; Ginsburg, 2007). Parental dedication to producing the perfect child is exhausting and little time remains for unscheduled and carefree playtime where children learn invaluable social and emotional lessons from each other. Children can also be deprived of much needed quality time with parents. With such a scarcity of downtime, even homework, which should be an opportunity for parents to bond and share in their children's school life, can become a stressful time.

Ironically, despite the busyness of most children's lives, the cry of 'I'm bored!' is commonly heard. Often parents respond by supplying instant gratification through games and other material possessions to ensure the child's happiness. However, no computer game or ritzy object can equal the social and emotional intelligence children gain from quality time with parents and from being with other children and creating their own entertainment, particularly in the natural environment. Health experts worry about children suffering from 'nature deficit disorder' where a lack of access to natural environments results in higher rates of physical and emotional illnesses (Sutterby, 2009). Immunologists refer to the hygiene hypothesis that advocates that today's children have more allergies than ever before, including life-threatening anaphylactic reactions to certain foods. This is mainly because, as young children, they have not been exposed to germs or a variety of foods and rough-and-tumble outdoor games that would have strengthened their immunity (Liu & Murphy, 2003).

> *Parents of this bubble-wrap generation seem to have an unrealistic fear of the natural world. They are reluctant to let their children get dirty, experience wild places or even take their shoes off and this biophobia deprives children of invaluable opportunities to learn skills, develop creativity and take risks.*
>
> **TRACY YOUNG, FACULTY OF HIGHER EDUCATION, SWINBURNE UNIVERSITY**

School newsletters can remind parents that giving children time to enjoy the complete freedom of unsanitised child-driven play increases their mental and physical health, creativity, resilience and confidence.

Finally, due to better nutrition, children today are physically growing up more quickly. While this is not inherently harmful, it can cause great angst for children who are emotionally unprepared to handle these physical changes. Teachers and parents must be ready to offer sensitive support to early and late developers who can look awkward and be vulnerable to a drop in self-esteem.

> *Puberty is arriving earlier and earlier. The average age for the onset is 10.75 years in girls and 11.5 years in boys. Children who reach puberty early face immense difficulties because they stand out from their peers. For girls, the surge of female hormones arrives at a time when their brain isn't ready for it. Children at that age are normally into fantasy play and the brain changes triggered by puberty are all about reality. It's very confusing for young children, and they often react by becoming withdrawn rather than precocious.*
>
> **PETER HINDMARSH, PROFESSOR OF PAEDIATRIC ENDOCRINOLOGY, GREAT ORMOND STREET HOSPITAL FOR CHILDREN, LONDON**

The world for children today is in so many ways cushioned but fast-moving, information-packed, anxiety-driven and technologically-enhanced. Teachers must remember that although children sitting in their classes are influenced by all of this, they still have the same basic needs that children have had for centuries: they need love, security, patience, time to have fun and grow at their own pace.

three

The social and emotional world of children

The role of the family

Children arrive at school carrying genetic and environmental treasures and wounds. Some arrive bursting with excitement, confidence and high levels of social and emotional intelligence because they have been blessed with wonderful families, in all manner of shapes and sizes. Others struggle to conceal situations and issues that no child should face. Teachers enjoy the privileged task of ensuring every child feels valued, needed and able to develop a sense of self-worth despite any home adversity. Unless this is achieved, even the most gifted teacher will be unable to help children thrive.

As Goleman (1996, pp. 189–190) states:

Family life is our first school for emotional learning; in this intimate cauldron we learn how to feel about ourselves and how others will react to our feelings; how to think about these feelings and what choices we have in reacting; how to read and express hopes and fears. This emotional schooling operates not just through the things that parents say and do directly to children, but also in the models they offer for handling their own feelings and those that pass between husband and wife. Some parents are gifted emotional teachers, others atrocious.

Modern families

The role of the family in shaping the social and emotional development of children remains fundamentally important; however, family structures have undergone unprecedented change over the last 20 years. With rising levels of divorce and family break-up, the number of single-parent or blended families has increased, placing many children in changing home situations. Change is always difficult for children. Young children whose families disintegrate will need additional teacher support because their cognitive and emotional immaturity often leads them to blame themselves for marital conflict (Ablow et al., 2009). Whether families separate or remain intact, ongoing parental conflict is very distressing for children and adversely affects all aspects of their lives including self-esteem, behaviour, academic achievement and overall wellbeing (Parkinson & Kazzi, 2011).

The increase in one-child families and in the number of children born to older parents has perhaps contributed to the greater incidence of intense parenting to 'get it right' for that one precious child. These parents may either have unrealistically high expectations, which can place pressure on children, or may be reluctant to provide important boundaries, which can result in children developing a sense of entitlement. Teachers should also be aware that some children are being raised by one parent and a grandparent or even grandparents alone. Grandparent-headed families are one of the fastest growing forms of out-of-home care for Australian children with approximately 30 000 children being raised entirely by their grandparents (Horner et al., 2007). Another form of family, that has only recently been discussed more openly, is the family composed of same-sex parents. Decades of research has shown no difference in the potential of homosexual and heterosexual parents to raise happy and healthy children with high self-esteem and well-developed social and emotional intelligence (Perrin, 2002). All family structures are valid and can provide the warmth and nurturing children deserve. It is important for teachers to acknowledge and show an acceptance of all family types. However, it is particularly important to show an inclusion and acceptance of same-sex parents if all children are to feel affirmed and included in class activities and special days where families are the focus. Unacceptably high levels of homophobia are present in many schools (Hillier et al., 2010), but teachers can mitigate the effects of stigmatisation and discrimination, which adversely affect children of gay parents, by promoting acceptance of difference.

Out of economic necessity many parents work long hours and constantly feel guilty about having inadequate time to spend with their children. These parents then compensate by buying their children material goods or by being reluctant to enforce adequate boundaries at home, which teach children valuable social and emotional norms. Ironically, children see *time* with their family as far more important than material possessions (Mori & Nairn, 2011). Technology has also introduced new layers of complexity into family life that can further erode quality time between parents and children. Due to mobile technology devices which provide 24/7 contact, today's parents are more 'connected' than ever before to work, as well as to friends, school and other parents. This can have a downside. Many teachers will have noticed the parent at a presentation night or sporting event who is engrossed in checking and sending text messages.

Technology is increasingly impacting on families. Sometimes parents should unplug and plug into their families a bit more. Some may think that being at the playground is spending quality time with their children, but if they are playing a game on their phone or doing work, they are not present. Children may feel they are not important if parents are constantly distracted. Having phones or social networking sites within reach can send children the message that parents are waiting for someone more important to communicate with them. Technology becomes the third 'person' in the room. Imagine the reaction of a parent if their teen texted at the table. Children learn what they see! Parents must model appropriate technological etiquette with children, switch off their phones and switch on to being fully present with their children.

SALLY-ANNE MCCORMACK, CHILD PSYCHOLOGIST

Schools must be sensitive to the pressures facing families. Maintaining close communication with parents can help even the busiest parents remain informed and emotionally involved in their children's education. This is extremely important as it allows parents to demonstrate interest in their children during these vitally important years when children look to parents for affirmation and validation.

Parents today are also struggling to absorb the plethora of information on parenting. Well-meaning, but constant, media attention on parenting often increases pressure on tired and confused parents who see their role as solving all problems and organising all things. Doherty (2000, p. 9) concludes that we have the 'most child-sensitive generation of parents the world has ever known – and the most confused and insecure'. Afraid to exercise any authority, and deferring to their children's wishes, many parents allow children to 'become the centre of their own insecure universe' (p. 9).

Rather than harming or restricting children, age-appropriate boundaries provide the security and safety net children need to test unfolding social and emotional wings. Children, with few boundaries at home, often come to school with an overextended sense of entitlement that rarely endears them to teachers or peers. These children must learn to fit into the school community by respecting social expectations. Teachers will need to patiently explain that classroom rules and structures must be adhered to for the good of the whole class.

From time to time various families will suffer severe setbacks. Stressed, disappointed, sad or angry parents impact enormously on their children's social and emotional development. Students behaving badly at school or suddenly producing substandard work may be in difficult family situations, such as navigating the trauma of losing a loved one. Teachers who are aware of children's home situations can offer more sensitive and appropriate support and provide a safe place at school when life at home is chaotic.

Effects of different parenting styles

While teachers cannot alter entrenched parenting styles, an understanding of these can help to explain rather than excuse students' behaviour. Baumrind (1966) identified three main parenting styles: authoritarian, authoritative and permissive. These are still recognised as having validity today.

Authoritarian parents demand blind obedience of strict rules with no explanation or exception to these rules. Infringements result in punishment. Children of these 'because I said so' parents are often obedient at school but are rarely as happy, confident or socially and emotionally competent as other children whose parents are less authoritarian.

Authoritative parents also establish rules and boundaries but these are explained. They are willing to listen to their children, encourage them to express an opinion and are warm and forgiving rather than punitive. These parents also encourage children to talk about their feelings and to respect others. Children of these parents are often happier, independent, assertive and more socially responsible. At school they are unafraid to face new challenges, are well-behaved and academically successful.

Permissive parents make few demands of their children, often indulging them due to tiredness or lack of time. Although they are generally nurturing, these parents behave more as friends to children than parents. Children need boundaries to provide a sense of security and children of permissive parents are often less happy. At school they are less willing to respect teacher authority because they get away with bad behaviour at home. They also often perform poorly at school.

Many researchers also mention *uninvolved* parenting (Kawabata et al., 2011). Although most teachers would identify few uninvolved parents, the effect on children is pervasive. Uninvolved parents are often overwhelmed by health and other personal issues and are simply unable to parent well. Emotionally detached from their children, they show them little warmth or love and often don't attend school events or parent–teacher meetings. Children of uninvolved parents must fend for themselves. They often have low self-esteem, are anxious or emotionally withdrawn, lack self-control and misbehave at school as there are few boundaries at home. Lacking the love and nurturing other children enjoy, they have poor social and emotional health and generally do not perform well academically.

Children blessed with parenting that is sensitive, consistent and warm but firm, develop higher self-esteem, self-control and follow social rules. The same applies in the classroom. Regardless of the parenting style children experience at home, teachers can provide the security and safety children need to develop greater social and emotional health. Sometimes school is the only place some children can experience a high level of emotional, and even physical safety and security. This knowledge can prompt tired teachers to persevere with patience and warmth, day after day, to nurture some children's fragile self-esteem.

Harnessing parent power: Strategies to support children's social and emotional development

▶ Information evenings and newsletter articles can offer parents advice and insights into issues affecting the social and emotional development of children while affirming the essential role they play. Enticing titles increase attendance, for example: 'Secrets to making children happier and more engaged at school'. Consider providing parents with the opportunity to email 'Burning questions and concerns' prior to the evening.

▶ A quick note, email or phone call can nip misunderstandings in the bud and strengthen parent–teacher relationships while providing opportunities to praise children's efforts and achievements. When parents see that they are valued as partners in their children's education, they report higher levels of satisfaction with teachers and their children enjoy better results, improved overall wellbeing and behaviour, higher academic aspirations and improved school attendance (Anfara, 2008).

▶ Work to ensure your school is parent-friendly and makes parents feel welcome. Be aware that some parents have time and employment pressures, cultural differences, a fear of authority-based institutions, ill health and other family issues that can impact on their ability to attend school functions. Many of these barriers can be overcome through frequent and warm communication with parents.

▶ Parent–teacher interviews are ideal opportunities to focus on more than academic results and to highlight children's social and emotional strengths. Be prepared and positive but deliver expectations and concerns clearly. Ask parents how they handle issues, particularly if the behaviour under discussion is negative.

▶ Build into homework tasks the opportunity for non-stressful and enjoyable parental involvement. Children could be required to interview a parent and ask questions like: 'What was your school like? What subjects did you study? What were the teachers like?' Children enjoy asking parents these questions. Consider inviting parents to present brief talks about their experiences.

The role of friends and peers

Learning to make and keep friends and find acceptance with peers is arguably the most important task of childhood and requires a healthy mix of socio–emotional skills. It is integral to children's ability to successfully negotiate the inevitable hurdles of childhood, adolescence and even life as an adult. Friends and peer acceptance bring a sense of validation and connectedness to school and help children to thrive academically, socially and emotionally. It is critical that teachers help children acquire strong friendship-making skills as early as possible (see Chapter 8). The ability to establish positive social relationships is one of the strongest predictors of happiness in children (Argyle, 2001). It provides an invaluable buffer for at–risk children exposed to stressful, negative and even hostile family situations, including punitive parental discipline and maltreatment (Criss et al., 2002; Hughes & Kwok, 2006). Teachers will have witnessed the healing energy and support that friendship and peer acceptance brings to children, particularly those in less than ideal circumstances. Children unable to establish friendships and positive relationships experience loneliness, escalating levels of disruptive behaviour and disengagement with school, and are more vulnerable to depression (Rubin et al., 2006). They may also be at higher risk of victimisation because they lack support in the face of aggressors (Bollmer et al., 2005). Having even one friend can protect rejected or victimised children against loneliness (Jobe-Shields et al., 2011). Sadly, as high as 10 per cent of primary children experience substantial loneliness, which undermines their mental health, wellbeing, enjoyment of school and perceived competence (Coplan et al., 2007).

For younger children, friendship is about casual fun and enjoyment. However, children approaching adolescence spend more time in organised activities or just 'hanging out' together where intimacy in friendship increases and becomes a source of affection. Peers are important for children from the earliest years but become their central preoccupation as adolescence approaches and peer acceptance equates with being 'normal'. Positive relationships with peers promote emotional wellbeing, motivation and academic achievement (Stewart, 2008). Teachers need to identify children relegated to the fringe of the peer group and help them refine important social skills. While friends are important to children, it is a lack of peer acceptance that has a more damaging impact on children's immediate and future wellbeing (Klima & Repetti, 2008). Research has also long shown that girls place more importance on intimacy and peer relationships and are more distressed by relational conflicts than boys (Crick, 1995). Teachers need, therefore, to be very thoughtful when supporting girls in conflict with peers.

Many young girls of primary age who face the crucial rite of passage to high [secondary] school seem bewildered by the precariousness of their friendship groups. My study of friendships in girls aged 10 to 14 revealed that primary school-aged girls tended to be regarded as compliant and conforming. In reality, however, many girls will hang on to the leader or the 'popular girl' within a friendship group even if the relationship is destructive and emotionally risky. Girl leaders are invariably bright, socially skilled and charismatic, and they have an unquestioning following because for girls on the periphery of the group, the alternative is being isolated, having no one to talk to, no one to play with, no one to walk home with. Furthermore, the girl leader who controls the group sets a moral code based on her version of loyalty that all have to adhere to and if you break the code, 'you're out!'. The girls in the study invested as much time in presenting themselves as nice and caring to adults as they did in their covert forms of bullying. Nevertheless, it was distressing to see that some teachers don't recognise the damage created by manipulative friendships and they too are taken in by the girl leaders whose exclusionary behaviours are not visible and usually take place below the radar.

**ROSALYN GEORGE, PROFESSOR OF EDUCATION
AND EQUALITY, UNIVERSITY OF LONDON**

The message is clear; every teacher in every class must look long and searchingly at the seemingly 'nice' and 'charming' girls – and boys – to ensure they are what they appear to be. Smiling faces of the 'good' girls can hide dangerous and manipulating behaviour. An excellent book highlighting the hidden world of girls' friendships and aggression is *Odd girl out* (Simmons, 2002). As Simmons cautions, not all 'friendships' are healthy. Teachers can help children form healthy friendships (see Chapter 8) that give them energy, inner strength and vitality rather than toxic alliances that can cause deep emotional scars. *Girls in a goldfish bowl* (George, 2007) is another important book that deepens our understanding of the high emotional investment girls make in friendships. This book highlights the exclusionary and inclusionary practices that characterise girls' complex friendships and examines the important role teachers can play in supporting preadolescent girls as they confront power-wielding 'friends'.

The role of teachers, school climate, culture and environment

Teachers

Teachers have enormous power to improve children's lives. Even seemingly small gestures and words of encouragement can have a lifelong impact on children. Teachers can model and explicitly teach social and emotional skills that can transform children's lives. They can make school a haven for children with unhappy and stressful home situations. Around 40 per cent of young people nominate teachers as significant people they would turn to in times of need (Arnon et al., 2008). Extensive research identifies the quality of the relationship between teachers and children as the most crucial element affecting children's overall experiences at school (Rowe, 2003). Teachers who frequently have meaningful conversations with children establish important connections with them and promote more positive social interactions among children (Cadima et al., 2010). Those who are warm and sensitive to children's needs, particularly in the early years, positively affect their current and future academic, social and behavioural outcomes. A positive relationship with a teacher can result in decreased levels of aggression and can promote peer acceptance, which is crucial for children's emotional development (Dockett & Perry, 2007; Hughes & Kwok, 2006).

It is widely acknowledged that when children like their teachers they generally want to please them, work harder and enjoy increased academic success (Graziano et al., 2007). Many incorrectly assume that academic success leads to a greater sense of belonging at school, when the central factor influencing student connectedness is the presence of caring peers and teachers (Ma, 2003). People, not results, lead to children feeling 'at home' in our schools. Children are remarkably perceptive and instantly detect when teachers have their welfare at heart. When teachers successfully earn children's trust through demonstrating their genuine concern, they create what Vygotsky termed the 'zone of proximal development' (ZPD), which facilitates children's optimal intellectual, social and emotional development (Levykh, 2008).

A teacher affects eternity; he can never tell where his influence stops.

HENRY ADAMS (1907/1999, P. 252)

Positive relationships with teachers are the foundation upon which children can build stronger social and emotional skills. In essence, teachers can transform the way children feel about themselves and the way they see the world and their future.

School climate

School plays a key role in the socialisation of children because school is their major social world during their formative years. School climate refers to the warmth and friendliness factor in schools. Great schools create communities where children feel safe, cared about and able to work together respectfully to solve problems. They give students an integral role to play in developing classroom expectations, which ensures their school is a warm and safe place. Empowering children to feel an ownership of their school engenders a genuine desire to protect it and the people in it, and reduces bullying (Birkett et al., 2009). Connectedness to school makes children happier, more resilient and even protects them against mental health issues, such as depression (Spence et al., 2005). Connectedness also improves children's academic results and increases socially acceptable behaviour (Stewart, 2008). Maslow's well-known Hierarchy of Needs (1962) highlights the importance of 'belonging' before other needs, such as self-esteem and personal achievement, can be attained. Children, who feel they are valued and belong at school, are socially, emotionally and academically advantaged.

Children have the right to learn in an enriching, safe school environment, so our Kids on Problem Solving (K. O. P. S.) program was formed to identify ways to make our school an even better place. K. O. P. S. fosters the development of effective social and decision-making skills and offers supportive relationships and team experiences that honour the school's values of mutual respect, caring and tolerance. Student-elected members aim to solve problems arising in the school and celebrate the uniqueness of each individual. They encourage their peers to respond to issues like bullying, using strategies such as 'ignore, walk away and report' and also volunteer their time to organise engaging games and activities during recess and lunchtime. K. O. P. S. members are encouraged to feel a positive emotional connection to students, teachers, support staff and their wider community. They are very proud to have this role and have developed better attitudes at school and higher self-esteem due to the responsibilities attached to it. We are proud of their contribution to making our school a place where every member enjoys the right to be respected and to be safe.

DONNA TEVEN, PRIMARY TEACHER

School culture

The culture of a school is more important than state-of-the-art facilities, school size, status, academic results or geographical location. How a school views itself, its values, assumptions, beliefs, practices and the way people in the school think, all form its culture. School policies, newsletters, public presentations, parent-school partnerships and interactions between staff and students reflect the true culture and what is valued. In essence it is 'the way we do things here' (Fullan & Hargreaves, 1996, p. 37). Schools with strong, positive cultures focus on academic, social and emotional outcomes for their students. Social and emotional learning programs pave the way for better academic learning and cognitive development. In the ideal learning environment, children are focused, fully attentive, motivated and engaged and enjoy their work (Zins et al., 2004). Schools that promote values of respect, acceptance and care, and actively work to develop emotionally literate learning environments, increase school connectedness for their students. This significantly enhances young people's resilience, prosocial behaviour, as well as their learning outcomes (Roffey, 2008).

Classroom teachers are influenced by school culture. Positive cultures empower individual teachers and provide them with a shared vision for the best outcomes for children while promoting strong professional relationships between staff, and between teachers and students. No matter what the culture of a school may be, it is now widely recognised that the individual teacher makes the greatest difference to outcomes, both academically and emotionally, for children in their classroom (Rowe, 2003). Children thrive and strive when teachers have positive relationships with them. Classroom teachers can make a difference to children in their care, even if their school has a negative or unhappy whole-school culture.

Parents often mention the culture of a classroom. They compare one teacher's style to another and the influence this has on their child. They notice the general classroom behaviour and the enthusiasm their child shows for wanting to go to school and for learning. Building positive classroom cultures and climates does not always depend on professional experience. Intuitive, committed graduate teachers can also engender classroom cultures of learning, cooperation and the desire to achieve. The spirit of a classroom – which includes: orderliness; vibrant displays of student learning; good manners and cooperation; well-articulated high expectations; regular praise to make children feel supported and valued; and well-informed parents who feel included – will be one whose culture results in a dynamic learning community.

By being supportive and building relationships, a classroom teacher can build a community where each child can feel safe to be a risk-taker while learning social and emotional skills. When children make mistakes or act inappropriately, conversations need to be one-to-one, treated with discretion and give children the opportunity to discuss fully the reasons why they misbehaved. This helps children find the best solutions for future situations. Classroom teachers should both protect and advocate for children and are the most important factor in making school a positive experience for them. Strong school and classroom cultures are developed through consistency, authenticity, care and ongoing professional learning; all of which should centre on the best outcomes for each child. Children will want to come to school when they feel safe and supported in their endeavours, and feel a sense of achievement.

Physical school environment

Whether the school is new or old, the care that staff and children show for school facilities reflects their pride in, and connectedness to, their school. A school which is clean, well cared for and inviting is a good environment in which a learning community can flourish. It reflects the respect and warmth between students and teachers and supports children's social and emotional growth. Teachers have the responsibility to ensure that their classrooms are safe, attractive, vibrant and well organised for optimal learning and relationship building. The classroom reflects the value teachers place on children by having their names, birthday charts and work displayed. This gives children a sense of belonging to the class. A classroom can be a home away from home where children feel comfortable, safe and inspired to learn and relate respectfully to others.

Experts have also found that schoolyards, resembling the more naturalistic settings children enjoyed in past generations, allow children's innate spirit of adventure and curiosity to thrive.

Bubble-wrapped children are being robbed of the chance to learn crucial life skills because school playgrounds are often uninspiring places where children are strictly controlled. In uninteresting playgrounds, with few possibilities for creative and imaginative play, bullying and behaviour issues are more common. The playground is where children develop and practise social skills, maths, science and environmental understandings through many types of self-directed play including rough-and-tumble, tree climbing, playing with loose natural materials and cubby building. Children need room to run and explore and freedom to learn through trial and error in playgrounds that cater for a wide range of play experiences. Teachers should set limits, but not be afraid of some risk-taking. Playgrounds need to meet safety standards but should not be devoid of interesting and challenging experiences.

**DR BARBARA CHANCELLOR, SENIOR LECTURER,
SCHOOL OF EDUCATION, RMIT UNIVERSITY**

Strategies to strengthen relationships with children

▶ Know the children. Initiate a structure where each child has a 10 to 15 minute meeting with the teacher at least twice each term. This allows time to chat with children about their families, interests and friends, and establish stronger relationships with them. Children also love hearing teachers share appropriate information about themselves. Even telling children that you also loved sport when you were at school can be seen as a cherished piece of information. These conversations establish trust with children.

▶ Develop empathic listening. This involves more than hearing, interpreting and responding. It is consciously placing oneself in children's reality and seeing the world through their eyes. Covey (1990, p. 241) states that:

Empathic listening is so powerful because it gives you accurate data to work with. Instead of projecting your own autobiography and assuming thoughts, feelings, motives and interpretation, you're dealing with the reality inside another person's head and heart.

▶ A teacher's ability to connect emotionally with children can be enhanced by reflecting on their own formative childhood experiences, be they positive or negative. Delve into your own memories of childhood. Some experiences are universal regardless of time or place.

▶ Be observant and listen to children with ears and eyes. You may discover valuable clues that a child claiming to be happy is deeply troubled or hiding fear or sadness (Borg, 2008; Engleberg & Wynn, 2010). Observe facial expressions, posture, tone of voice, hands fidgeting or an unwillingness to make eye contact. Only 7 per cent of a message is understood from spoken words, 38 per cent from the *way* those words are spoken combined with other body language clues, while 55 per cent is derived from facial expressions (Mehrabian, 1981).

▶ Become familiar with the world children inhabit. Know the television programs, websites, chat rooms, music and heroes they admire. Try to keep up with the latest jargon and buzz words. Good luck!

PART TWO

Emotional development

four

Foundations of emotional development

Teachers can make children excited and curious about the whole world of emotions by telling them that they will discover the secrets to:

- be stronger and more in control of their *own* thoughts and actions because they can identify and understand how they feel
- get along better with others, be more popular and make friends more easily because they can identify and understand how *other* people feel
- be more successful at school and in future situations and careers because they will be masters of themselves.

Children love hearing that they will learn to understand a whole new world: the world of emotional intelligence.

Recognising, naming and understanding feelings

Children who recognise and name their feelings can decode their emotional world and begin understanding and mastering emotions rather than being enslaved by them. This is a crucial task for children in the early primary years. Research highlights the importance of parents talking to young children about feelings (Brazelton & Sparrow, 2005); however, many children are not fortunate enough to have this experience at home. They are often unaware that uncomfortable, and sometimes frightening, feelings are common emotions everyone can learn to recognise and control. At school, these children face a confusing emotional maze that hampers their ability to thrive in every sense. Teachers can be important role models who teach children the language of feelings and how to express these in a healthy way. In other words, even the simple act of naming how a child feels and how that makes others feel can be a wonderful example of how to handle emotions well. For example: 'Julie, I know you feel frustrated, but when you scribble on someone else's work, we all feel sad'. Vygotsky, eminent psychologist and educator, saw emotions as being an integral part of the very fabric of teaching and learning. In reflecting on Vygotsky's work, Levykh (2008, p. 92) states:

> ... *successful learning begins when teachers exhibit a sense of emotional openness, especially at the initial stage of teaching. Such openness facilitates a sense of wonder among students and stimulates their imagination and, thus, enhances the process of learning.*

Children who learn to recognise and understand their own emotions can then begin to appreciate the emotions of others. They acquire empathy, which is an invaluable social attribute. It is important to remember that despite enormous setbacks or personal hurdles, all children can learn to be better masters of their emotions (Raver, 2004). Children model what they see and hear, both from teachers and their first educators: parents.

We've always talked about feelings in our family. Even when he was a baby I would help Tom change his mood if I noticed something was wrong. If he was upset, I would distract him by taking him outside and walking around the garden. As Tom got older, if we argued and he got angry, I taught him how to deal with it by controlling my own anger. I named my emotions so he understood how I felt: 'I'm feeling tired right now, so I'm sorry if I sound cranky but I really need to get this done. Can we talk when I'm finished and I'm in a better mood?'

When a close friend I'd known for 30 years died, I went into the bedroom after I got the phone call and started to cry. Tom came into the room. I explained what had happened and said that I was very sad and needed to have a good cry until I felt ready to come out again. He was only about 4 but he seemed to understand and left me alone. In later years Tom realised that he could have a good cry too and then scoop himself up again. We never told him to shut up or called him a sook. We let him deal with feelings and then move on rather than bottling them up or dragging the family down with moodiness. He's now 12 and can manage his feelings and not just be a victim of them or inflict them carelessly on others.

KIMBERLY, MOTHER OF TOM, 12

Strategies to help children recognise, name and understand feelings

▶ Teach children to identify the messages hidden in body language. While using a blank mask that only shows the eyes, children can mime various feelings. This helps them become more attuned to body language. By then removing the mask and acting out a feeling, children can gain a greater appreciation of the power of facial expressions.

▶ Art is a very therapeutic way to help children express their feelings. Provide cardboard, material, glue and other resources so that children can make masks or pictures illustrating particular feelings. Have children present to the class while others guess the illustrated feelings.

▶ Encourage children to discuss feelings in circle time so that everyone has an opportunity to contribute and be heard. For example: 'What does anger/happiness/sadness look like? What does it feel like?' (see Chapter 6).

▶ Display photos of people experiencing various feelings. Give students labels (sad, frightened, angry, happy, surprised, worried, excited, embarrassed, disappointed and confused) and ask them to work in groups and attach the appropriate labels.

▶ Picture storybooks and literature can open, touch and inspire young minds by giving children opportunities to explore feelings through characters.

Managing and expressing feelings

Children who understand and articulate their feelings are then more able to manage and communicate these to others. This is an important developmental task for children to achieve. Gaining self-control gives them a greater ability to build friendships, which is fundamental to children's happiness. The ability to manage emotions is also strongly linked to academic success and better relationships with peers and teachers (Graziano et al., 2007). Because Australia is such a multicultural society, teachers can avoid misunderstandings by considering the impact cultural background and traditions may have on children's emotional regulation and expression. These may differ markedly from behaviour taken for granted in the mainstream culture. In America, another multicultural country, Campos et al. (2004, p. 384) state:

> *In this country, temperamental inhibition is not highly valued; most of us prefer our children to be assertive, bold and sociable. Consequently, we often link temperamental*

inhibition to emotional dysregulation. In China, by contrast, temperamentally inhibited children are valued. Shyness is considered to be an indication of a willingness to obey the rules of the culture, of being studious and hard working, and of keeping his or her place in the culturally prescribed order of status.

Strategies to help children manage and express feelings

▶ Reassure children that being able to handle emotions is a learning journey rather than a test of what is right and wrong. Stress that it's okay to make mistakes. Everyone makes mistakes, even teachers, and this is all a part of learning.

▶ Encourage children to recognise and talk about how feelings affect their body. For example: 'How does anger or fear make you feel? Hot or cold, prickly, sweaty or dizzy?' When children learn to recognise physiological signs, they are ready to consider ways to manage them.

▶ Help children identify how particular feelings make them behave. Do they act aggressively, avoid eye contact or make inappropriate comments? Teach children that it's normal to feel emotions like anger and fear, but it's not acceptable to react by hurting others or damaging property. Children need to hear that it takes courage, strength and intelligence to handle strong emotions well.

▶ Support children to identify a range of coping strategies and behaviours when faced with difficult feelings. Help them by asking questions like: 'Who could you speak to? What is the best way to respond?' Effective strategies include counting to 10 slowly, moving away rather than lashing out or visualising a safe place in which to calm down and think rationally.

▶ Help children identify thoughts that accompany feelings. Some children tend to have negative thoughts pulling them down into dark places where they instinctively lash out in an effort to protect themselves. Explain that people of all ages successfully use self-talk as a form of armour in tricky or challenging situations. Children enjoy hearing that even famous sports idols use self-talk to empower themselves mentally before important events. You could ask children to think of situations where self-talk could help (e.g. bullying, unfamiliar social situations or preparing for tests) or to write a list of their own powerful self-talk. Encourage children to practise these privately. In Chapter 5 we discuss teaching children to challenge automatic negative thoughts that often rush into their heads producing strong and potentially frightening emotions.

▶ Ask children to write about happy or difficult feelings, achievements and even setbacks in a reflective journal. These can be shared with the teacher if children wish. Writing about feelings is very therapeutic.

▶ Model expressing and handling emotions well. Children are remarkably perceptive and notice how teachers respond to situations (Newberry & Davis, 2008).

▶ Display a poster reminding children how to manage feelings.

CLASSROOM POSTER

How to manage feelings:

▶ WHAT am I feeling?

▶ WHY am I having this feeling?

▶ HOW can I manage this feeling well?

▶ WHO can give me advice?

▶ CHOOSE the best action and TAKE CONTROL.

Self-concept

Self-concept is widely accepted as being the foundation of social and emotional development (Woolfolk & Margetts, 2010). Self-concept is the picture we have of ourselves. For example: 'I am not very tall. I am very good at sport. I am not good at maths ...' Children are constantly refining their self-concept as they receive feedback – positive or negative – from important people around them. School experiences have a huge impact on children's self-concept, especially for those who do not receive affirmation from home. Right from the first years at school, children are forming opinions about their abilities and limitations as they constantly refine their sense of personal identity. Children want to fit in and find acceptance from peers and this desire intensifies yearly until it becomes the major preoccupation of preadolescents and adolescents.

Strategies to help children develop a healthy self-concept

▶ Children who feel different can develop negative self-concepts. Encouraging an acceptance of difference – be it cultural, physical or family differences – helps children begin to see difference as special rather than something to be ashamed of.

▶ Producing a family tree or investigating the life of one special family member helps children establish a deeper sense of belonging, which aids self-concept and identity development. Allowing children to choose how they present their family protects those who may not want to fully reveal their family situation.

▶ Encourage a cooperative classroom by assigning roles (e.g. scribe, organiser or presenter) where children will shine and can use their strengths: 'Tom, I want you to be group leader because you're a born organiser'. Avoid placing children in positions where they may 'fail' such as asking poor readers to read aloud. Subtly choose less difficult passages and have children rehearse these before class or public presentations.

▶ Help students accept their limitations while identifying and developing their strengths. Some children don't recognise their own strengths and capabilities.

Self-esteem

Self-concept is the picture we have of ourselves, while self-esteem is how we *feel* about this picture. Children's self-esteem develops as they taste success and confidence is nurtured. Self-esteem is a work in progress and can be strengthened by teacher praise for effort and success. High self-esteem gives children the confidence to attempt new challenges unhampered by the fear of failure. This applies equally to schoolwork, making new friends or taking part in school activities.

Erikson (1963) believed that children need to master the social and emotional challenges appropriate to their age in order to be ready to successfully tackle future challenges. In Stage 3 of Erikson's theory of psychosocial development, 'initiative vs. guilt', children from 3 to 5 begin to assert control and power over their environment, particularly through social interaction and play. Mastery leads to a sense of purpose, but failure to acquire appropriate social and emotional skills burdens children with a legacy of guilt, self-doubt and poor self-esteem. In Stage 4, 'industry vs. inferiority', children from 6 to 12 encounter new and wider social experiences requiring increased self-confidence and more developed social and emotional intelligence. During these important primary school years, children should be developing a sense of pride in their achievements and abilities through feedback from within their social world. Those who are encouraged by parents, teachers and peers develop vital feelings of competence and a positive self-belief. However, praise should focus more on *effort* than intelligence. This ensures that all children, from the strugglers to the high achievers, can gain a sense of personal achievement. Contrary to long-held belief, praising children's intelligence does not necessarily give them more confidence, higher self-esteem or help them learn more. Indeed, high achievers and gifted children can sometimes stop working to their full potential if they are constantly praised for their intelligence, rather than effort, because they begin to fear making mistakes and not living up to expectations (Dweck, 2006).

Undoubtedly, parenting style can affect children's self-esteem (see Chapter 3). Children with authoritarian parents typically have low self-esteem because they are not allowed to have choices, make decisions or express themselves (Peters Mayer, 2008). Children whose parents are authoritative, however, have healthy self-esteem because they grow up in families where parents are loving, accepting and where boundaries are clear and consistent, but not harsh. When parents are over-protective and discourage children's independence, children, particularly those who have a tendency to be insecure, begin to believe they are helpless and self-esteem suffers (Rubin et al., 2009). Although self-esteem first begins to form in the home, who can forget that first teacher who told you that you could be a singer or a mathematician! Teachers should never underestimate the enormous power they have to boost children's self-esteem and positively affect their immediate and long-term wellbeing.

Children with high self-esteem are more:

- popular, cooperative, independent and responsible
- resilient
- capable of handling emotions and developing good relationships
- positive about school
- protected from bullying
- able to reach their potential academically.

Danger spots that can erode children's self-esteem include:

> periods of change, such as starting school or transitioning to secondary school
> not succeeding academically
> unrealistically high parental expectations or highly critical parents
> bullying
> problems with school work
> lack of friends or alienation from the peer group
> feeling different or not fitting in.

NEWSLETTER ITEM

How to increase your child's self-esteem and confidence:

> Tell your child you love him or her. With busy lives, it's easy to overlook the most important words children need to hear.
> Show interest and help with your child's homework.
> Make time every day to ask about your child's day at school.
> Acknowledge your child's feelings, fears or dreams even if they appear to be exaggerated or trivial. For your child, these may be the stuff of nightmares.
> Show real interest in your child's interests, friends and day-to-day world. Can you name your child's best friends, favourite singers, actors and musical groups?
> Criticise behaviour, not your child.
> Listen and ask for your child's opinions.
> Praise your child's efforts as much as their achievements.
> Help your child develop new interests and therefore opportunities for success.
> Encourage age-appropriate independence and again praise effort. Walking or taking public transport to and from school is an important step for children. In addition to helping children acquire a sense of identity it boosts self-esteem, confidence and independence.
> Encourage your child's friends to visit your home.
> Know your child's teacher and develop a trusting relationship so that your child sees the teacher as being in partnership with you to maximise their best interests.

Strategies to increase children's self-esteem

▶ Identify and praise children's talents – personal, social, emotional and academic – but especially their efforts.

▶ Introduce the concept of 'multiple intelligences' to children (Gardner, 1993). Every child is strong in one of the intelligences: linguistic, logical-mathematical, musical, bodily-kinaesthetic, spatial or visual, interpersonal, intrapersonal, naturalistic or existential. Gifts may be well hidden, but teachers are generally great archaeologists when faced with unearthing children's special skills and attributes. Teachers will vividly remember children with high levels of interpersonal intelligence who could conduct visitors around the school with great self-assurance or the child who was a great sports person, yet these children struggled academically. Allowing children the opportunity to shine in areas where their talents lie builds self-esteem.

▶ Children need to know that teachers believe in them and have high expectations of them. Negative messages can result in a self-fulfilling prophecy. In a landmark study, children who knew their teachers had low expectations of them consequently developed low levels of self-perceived academic ability and low self-esteem (Phillips, 1984).

▶ Extra-curricular activities have been linked to better school results, which boosts self-esteem (Guest & Schneider, 2003). Help children step outside their comfort zone and face new challenges, again emphasising that effort is as highly valued as results. Carefully chosen challenges with a high chance of success help children get scores on the board.

▶ It is never too early to give children careers education (Magnuson & Starr, 2000; Proctor, 2005). This increases self-esteem and self-reflection while empowering children, facilitating identity formation and providing many other tangible benefits socially, emotionally and academically.

▶ Students with particularly low self-esteem may require a referral to a counsellor within or outside the school.

The greatest gift we can give children is the notion that they can be whatever they want to be. Yes, we must provide them with the basic skills of literacy, numeracy and curiosity, but without the main ingredient of having a sense of worth, high self-esteem and a positive outlook in life, all other efforts are wasted. One of the main foci of our personalised learning program is to increase student engagement and encourage children to think positively about their career options. Year 5 and 6 students meet members of our community from all walks of life and in different career settings. The aim of the visits is to illustrate that one's future is shaped by the present and that full involvement, participation and connection with the school community is the ideal start. A common theme heard and seen in our classrooms, corridors and school yard is 'Only my best will do'.

KAREN WILEMAN, PERSONALISED LEARNING TEACHER; TONY CERRA, PRIMARY PRINCIPAL

With the support of our local training company, we decided to give our Year 5 and 6 students a taste of a different profession each term. Students spend one afternoon a week over a 6-week-period exploring a career with industry tours, hands-on activities and guest speakers. Themes have included agriculture and horticulture, hospitality, construction and automotive studies. We also focus on life skills to give students a feeling for the responsibilities involved in various careers. Thinking about possible careers opens children's minds, raises expectations, broadens horizons and develops the self-belief that anything is possible. Early experiences enhance later life chances. The children love the program and it helps them develop an understanding that their education has a purpose.

KERYN ACKLAND, PRIMARY TEACHER

gress res
ation practice
ics foundation se

personal we
pathy individual progress
eing values co
five

Building blocks of emotional health

Resilience and optimism generally go hand in hand and are undoubtedly two of the most vital attributes for children to possess. They help children approach life with a give-it-a-go attitude and protect them from the debilitating effects of negativity. Teachers often experience the frustration of seeing children refuse or strongly resist participation in potentially fun-filled and confidence-building activities. Some begin activities lacking confidence and achieve little due to investing minimal effort. Each setback can deepen pessimism until children's expectation of failure becomes a reality. Due to positive or negative experiences at home, children arrive at school already possessing either an optimistic or a pessimistic outlook (Murray & Fortinberry, 2006). However, skilful and caring teachers can guide children to change their thinking and develop that wonderful glass-half-full attitude.

Optimism: Positive thinking and self-talk

Optimistic thinking cushions children from the impact of negative life situations (Spence et al., 2005) and leads to outcomes such as better moods, greater perseverance, success and better physical health (Seligman, 2000). It comes as no surprise that children's optimism thrives in an optimistic household (Murray & Fortinberry, 2006). Murray and Fortinberry identify five factors that contribute to children's optimism: (1) parents have a good relationship with their children; (2) parents spend quality time with their children; (3) parenting styles involve empathy and consistency; (4) there are shared family values; and (5) children have access to a challenging and natural environment. Children from families where there is constant conflict, or where parents work long hours and therefore have little time to spend with them, are less inclined to be optimistic. Teachers must be sensitive to home circumstances that may erode children's optimism.

Apart from greatly improving children's overall wellbeing, teaching children to think positively leads to a more optimistic frame of mind, which results in improved academic achievement and classroom behaviour. With optimism, levels of aggression, hyperactivity and impulsivity *decrease,* while prosocial behaviour, attentiveness and academic achievement *increase* (Fisher et al., 2004).

Seligman (2007, p. 7) describes pessimism as an 'entrenched habit of mind that has sweeping and disastrous consequences: depressed mood, resignation, underachievement, and even unexpectedly poor physical health'. Unmanaged pessimism can lead to clinical depression. Children who are negative possess a failure mentality and are so worried about impending disaster that they are distracted, prevented from concentrating in class and consequently miss a lot of information entirely (Cassady & Johnson, 2002). These are the children who give up before they have even begun. Teachers often struggle to motivate and engage these children but there are strategies that can assist these and all children to develop greater optimism and positive thinking.

Cognitive Behaviour Therapy (CBT) and other classroom strategies to teach positive thinking

Renowned American psychiatrist Aaron Beck and fellow researcher David Clark (2010) speak of 'catastrophic thinking' or the tendency to think and predict doom and gloom. This is an acquired habit that creates a low mood, saps energy and even produces the poor physical health associated with depression. But habits can be broken. Teachers can help children conquer negative and catastrophic patterns of thinking. In the 1960s, Beck and colleagues developed Cognitive Behaviour Therapy (CBT). This treatment approach involves helping others understand, manage and change their thoughts (cognitions) and consequently their actions (behaviour). In essence, negative thoughts are replaced with more realistic and positive thoughts. This is very effective in treating depression, anxiety, eating disorders, social phobia and other mental health issues and helps children develop an 'I can do it' mentality. With increasing levels of depression in children, it is reassuring that cognitive strategies are comparable with medication for treating mild clinical depression and superior to medication in preventing the return of depression (Goleman, 1996).

Teachers have successfully integrated CBT techniques into their teaching of emotional and social skills through programs such as FRIENDS (Barrett et al., 2000). FRIENDS is based on CBT and focuses on problem solving and social skills to address children's anxiety and depression. It is just one of the many programs available to classroom teachers (Neil & Christensen, 2007). An American program, Skills for Academic and Social Success (Fisher et al., 2004), helps students recognise that anxiety is maintained through negative thinking. Students are taught 'realistic thinking', adapted from Ronald Rapee's book *Overcoming shyness and social phobia* (1998). To prevent catastrophic thinking, students use specific questions to evaluate negative expectations more realistically. For example, 'Am I exaggerating? Is "X" really going to be the end of the world? What do other people do in this situation? What would I think if this happened to my friend?' These questions can be modified and used with students of all ages. Another strategy to help children is to ask: 'On a scale of 1 to 10 (where 10 is something really bad) can you give me an example of some things that are really bad?' Most children will mention events such as world disasters and the death or serious illness of loved ones. You could then ask: 'Now, where would you rank what has just happened to you?' This exercise helps all children, especially highly anxious children, to gain perspective, which is an important step towards more positive thinking.

CBT strategies are particularly effective when children are faced with stress, anxiety and perceived threats. Children need to identify what is stressing or threatening them (the 'nasties') before they can change their way of thinking to break the cycle of defeatism and negativity. Children often suffer from the 'deer-in-the-headlights' syndrome and freeze in the face of perceived threat or danger. Others lash out inappropriately as it's the only way they know to protect themselves. These children need support to become familiar with, and work through, 'thinking steps', which help them to think positively and behave in more socially-appropriate ways. Steps must be simple and easy if children are to remember them in stressful situations. Posters can be displayed in the classroom as constant reminders.

CLASSROOM POSTER

How to use thinking steps to crush the 'nasties':

▶ STOP!
▶ RELAX
▶ THINK
▶ ACT.

Explicitly teaching and reminding children of 'thinking steps' facilitates their social and emotional development and provides a good starting point for one-to-one conversations with children who speak or behave inappropriately. To demonstrate care and interest in children's feelings, begin by listening to them without interrupting. For example: 'Tell me your story. What happened?' The key is to tease out what has really happened and how children feel, before helping them evaluate their thoughts and behaviour. For example: 'Did you remember the "thinking steps" we talked about? Let's go through these together and work out what happened'. This is infinitely more positive and productive than saying, 'Can you explain your *behaviour*?' or even, 'Let's see if we can find another way you could have *behaved*.'

There are many excellent and readily available teacher resources, such as *Behavior management: Positive applications for teachers* (Zirpoli, 2010) and workbooks by Tony Attwood (2004a; 2004b), that guide teachers and schools in using CBT strategies with children. It is heartening that, with patience and practice, children can learn healthier ways of thinking, seeing the world and acting accordingly.

Self-talk

Many children tend to be plagued by negative self-talk, which erodes their self-confidence and ability to learn, socialise and enjoy school. Children can be taught to use *positive* self-talk. Teachers must first introduce children to the concept of an internal dialogue by explaining that we all 'talk' to ourselves, especially when we are afraid or nervous. For example: 'Everyone has these voice-thoughts, even adults and famous musicians and sports stars'. Children can then be presented with scenarios in which characters have negative thoughts. In groups they can replace the characters' negative self-talk with positive self-talk.

▷ 'I'll never win' → 'If I try hard I have a chance of winning'
▷ 'I am never going to pass this test' → 'I have worked hard. Nothing can stop me from doing my best'
▷ 'I'll look stupid when I do my talk' → 'Relax. I know this topic'
▷ 'Everyone will laugh at me' → 'My friends are on my side'.

Another powerful way to help children develop positive self-talk is through teacher modelling. Thinking out loud is an effective strategy appropriate for children of all ages. For example, you might say: 'I think I am going to take a deep breath. I am really frustrated that there is so much noise coming from the yard when we are trying to enjoy our class presentations. But I am going to ignore it and not let it spoil our class. Let's all face this way and enjoy the next talk.' When it becomes second nature for teachers to articulate positive self-talk in their daily interactions with children, children will often unconsciously emulate this positive approach to handling obstacles. Seeing teachers model self-talk, and not allowing feelings to upset them, teaches children a life-enriching lesson.

In his book *The optimistic child,* positive psychologist Martin Seligman (2007) outlines a 12-week program that teaches children to think positively, challenge and change negative 'automatic thoughts' that may pop into their heads. The program includes comic strips, role-plays, games, discussions and videos, which all appeal to children. While the program is recommended for 8- to 12-year-olds, it could be modified for younger or older children. In essence, this entertaining program engages children by allowing them to take on the role of detectives as they move through the following easy steps:

1. 'Thought catching' or recognising automatic thoughts such as, 'I'm dumb. Everyone hates me'.
2. Challenging the automatic thoughts and evaluating their accuracy: 'What real evidence do I have that this is true?' Children (and not infrequently adults) often believe their first negative thoughts but can learn that they do not have to accept these suspect thoughts.
3. The third step is to paint a more accurate picture or explanation: 'I'm not dumb. I just can't solve maths problems as fast as my friends'; 'Everyone doesn't hate me. Jason doesn't want to be my friend but I have other good friends'.

Display posters reminding children that they can master their thinking.

CLASSROOM POSTER

How to control my own put-downs:

- ▶ CATCH negative thoughts
- ▶ CHALLENGE them to a duel
- ▶ REJECT inaccurate and negative thoughts
- ▶ THINK POSITIVELY and ACCURATELY.

Building resilience

Resilience is the priceless ability to bounce back from setbacks and disappointments and move forwards positively despite adversity. Resilient children generally have strong social and emotional intelligence (Rae, 2006), problem-solving ability, autonomy and a sense of purpose and future possibilities (Hanewald, 2011). Understandably, they are happier and more confident than children lacking resilience. Teachers directly contribute to children's resilience by helping them develop all of these skills and outlooks through encouragement, explicit teaching and modelling.

While most teachers can identify children possessing resilience and those whose ability to thrive is hindered because of a lack of it, studies reveal that many teachers need a deeper understanding of resilience (Green et al., 2007; Russo & Boman, 2007). Given its complexity, this is not a criticism of teachers. Being familiar with research into resilience promotes teachers' understanding and ability to develop strategies to support all children, but especially those at risk. As with self-esteem, resilience is not a fixed attribute that children either possess or lack (Hanewald, 2011), although some children are genetically predisposed to being more resilient than others (Mandleco & Craig, 2000). Resilience is fragile and fluid. Teachers must be vigilant because even the most resilient children can fall in a heap when faced with particularly stressful life circumstances (Green et al., 2007).

The first step to increasing children's resilience is to help them understand and accept that no one succeeds all of the time. Children must learn that effort, perseverance and a willingness to give life a go are more valuable than winning or succeeding. Some well-intentioned parents prevent children from developing resilience by over-protecting them and not allowing them to confront difficult issues or obstacles. Resilience is developed by learning to 'fail' and picking oneself up again, time after time. Each decision to get back up again builds strength and character. As Seligman (2007, p. 45) states:

> *If we cushion feeling bad, and protect children from failure, we make it harder for them to truly appreciate feeling good and appreciating a true sense of mastery or achievement. In fact we create children vulnerable to depression because they have not learnt to handle setbacks and obstacles.*

Protective factors for resilience

Researchers highlight protective factors that can cushion children when facing life's inevitable hurdles and actively increase their resilience (Howard & Johnson, 2000; Minnard, 2002). Protective factors include: having a stable family environment and a high level of connectedness to that family; realistic parental expectations regarding academic performance; and membership of supportive organisations, such as churches, youth groups, sporting, musical or other community groups (Mandleco & Craig, 2000). Increasingly, research shows that having a spiritual or religious affiliation increases resilience by providing support and meaning in times of adversity, an opportunity to develop friendships and the security of belonging to a close-knit community (Cook, 2000; Regneruis & Elder, 2003). Whether employed in schools with a religious affiliation or not, all teachers can be open to acknowledging and affirming the role religion may play in the lives of some children. Children are spiritual beings (Bhagwan, 2009) and benefit from seeing a purpose and meaning in life and from the opportunity to explore spirituality. This can be achieved by guiding children to appreciate the beauty in nature, art, music, culture and other people.

Other protective factors that have particularly important implications for teachers include children: having an attachment to at least one significant adult (Oswald et al., 2003); experiencing a sense of achievement in a valued activity; experiencing some sense of success at school where teachers are warm and caring (Brooks & Goldstein, 2008; Hanewald, 2011); and forming and maintaining friendships and connectedness to peers (Nickolite & Doll, 2008). We know that teachers can be that significant person in many children's lives and also have the power to help children taste success and learn the skills to form positive relationships. A warm school climate also helps children feel connected to school, which enhances their resilience (Spence et al., 2005). The more protective factors children have, the more likely they are to be resilient.

Factors placing children at risk

Apart from an absence of protective factors, decades of research have identified various other negative factors that may place children at risk. Some of these include: a dysfunctional family life, including frequent changes in living arrangements; needing to look after siblings or parents (East, 2010); abuse of any form; witnessing violence within either the family or the community; socioeconomic disadvantage; separation or divorce; death of a loved person; and exposure to any form of severe adversity or trauma (Masten & Coatsworth, 1998). More than ever before, we are also aware that bullying and cyberbullying can place children at risk for depression, anxiety and even suicide (Beane, 2008; Wang et al., 2011). Some children may have a number of negative factors in their lives that are completely hidden from teachers. Being familiar with some of the signs that children may be at risk helps teachers come to their aid more quickly. Teachers should also consult with school leaders and welfare staff so that additional support strategies can be discussed for the most at-risk children.

SIGNS OF AT-RISK CHILDREN

- Poor social and emotional skills
- Withdrawn, aggressive or disruptive behaviour
- Unhappy or anxious
- Lacking friends or inability to find acceptance with peers
- Being different (this can make children more vulnerable to low self-esteem, anxiety, teasing, bullying and the many negative consequences these bring)
- Over-reliance on parents or teachers
- Frequent illness or absenteeism from school
- Frequently tired or unkempt appearance

Strategies to increase children's resilience

- Teachers should never underestimate their power to build children's resilience by establishing a nurturing and safe classroom climate and, above all, a strong relationship with children (Brooks & Goldstein, 2008). A warm relationship of trust with teachers is seen by many experts as the strongest protective factor operating in schools (Nickolite & Doll, 2008). A feeling of belonging and being valued enhances children's sense of self-worth and their ability to face obstacles and take risks in learning.

▶ Model a positive attitude to failure and setbacks. This is particularly important when many children do not have 'glass-half-full' outlooks modelled at home. Share personal stories or read picture storybooks featuring characters who have overcome setbacks.

▶ Make children aware that they will not be judged as inferior or less lovable if they fail, otherwise they will fear trying because of the possibility of not meeting expectations. Display inspirational quotes or posters around the classroom:

- *Fall seven times, get up eight.* (Japanese Proverb)
- *The first pancake is always a failure.* (Russian proverb)
- *Your failures could be stepping stones to success.* (American proverb)

▶ Explain that Thomas Edison invented the electric light bulb after more than 2000 experiments. When asked by a young reporter how it felt to fail so many times, he replied: 'I never failed once. I invented the light bulb. It just happened to be a 2000-step process' (Siccone & Canfield, 1993, p. 137).

▶ Through school newsletters, outline safe and age-appropriate challenges parents could provide to help children step outside their comfort zone and learn to adapt to new and challenging situations. Bolster the confidence and self-esteem of children whose parents harbour unrealistically high expectations of them or are constantly critical of results and behaviour.

▶ Well-tried and popular resources, such as *Bounceback* (McGrath & Noble, 2003), provide a sequential approach for teaching resilience.

six

Helping children handle negative emotions

When children reach school age, their coping skills and perceptions about feelings are already established through interaction with their parents and home environment (Goleman, 1996). Many will have good skills, appropriate to their age and developmental expectations. Others will reflect difficulties at home or have 'caught' parental fears and need special support and understanding.

> It was a surprise when Rebecca arrived new to the school in Year 4 and immediately baulked at entering the school building on her own. Her parents had not indicated they had any concerns. On Rebecca's first day, her parents, who appeared very anxious, just couldn't get her past the front door. Developmentally a child at this age would normally be seeking greater independence, yet we continued to have difficulty detaching her from her parents for several months. Only a handover at the school door to the principal, the receptionist or an available staff member worked. It was a real team effort. Slowly, with small negotiated steps and increased expectations, Rebecca was confident enough to get to the classroom by herself. It was a great success, achieved with a minimum of fuss so her classmates didn't really catch on at all! This was a child who really loved school when eventually she achieved separation from her anxious parents.
>
> **MARIA, PRIMARY SCHOOL PRINCIPAL**

Negative emotions such as fear, anger or grief are a normal part of the human experience. For children, however, an inability to understand and handle these emotions can be frightening, adversely affecting every aspect of their lives and leading to overriding anxiety. In particular, their ability to establish positive social relationships is severely hampered (Zeman &

Shipman, 1996). Children who cannot form positive relationships with peers and adults are prevented from achieving their best academically and do not find school as fulfilling as it should be. Emotions cannot be separated from learning. Unlike relaxed and positive emotions that release neurochemicals conducive to learning (Geake & Cooper, 2003), fear and anxiety reduce children's ability to learn by causing blood to flow away from the neocortex (the seat of cognitive processes). This can make children go blank, limiting them to those primitive responses that promote survival (Fredrickson & Branigan, 2005). In this fight or flight mode, the more sophisticated parts of the brain virtually shut down (Goleman, 1996). While small levels of stress can motivate children to dig deeper and face challenges, chronic stress is very different and can lead to anxiety that significantly damages physical and mental wellbeing (Healey, 2009). All teachers will remember children who emotionally explode or implode when confronted with upsetting or challenging situations. An inability to handle upsetting emotions prevents children from optimal learning and enjoyment of school (Panju, 2008). Teachers help enormously by recognising when children are feeling bad and helping them identify, understand and regulate negative emotions. This emotionally frees children to redirect valuable energy into learning, socialising and enjoying life. Unless they are supported in handling negative emotions, children's emotional stress can develop into clinical depression (see Chapter 11).

Validating 'uncomfortable' feelings

When children display negative or 'uncomfortable' emotions, it is important to teach them that these emotions are natural and normal and they are not bad people for feeling the emotions of anger, jealousy or aggression. The message children need is that it is all right to have feelings like anger, but the way we handle these feelings should not hurt or intimidate others. Although some children arrive at school with an inability to understand and manage difficult feelings, the rehabilitative work of caring teachers can make an enormous difference to their lives. Many adults may have saved a fortune on therapists if, as children, they had learnt to handle difficult feelings.

Children's emotional outbursts are opportunities for teachers to model effective management of emotions and to teach coping skills. For example:

This has been a difficult day. Let's talk about how we feel and discuss ways to feel
better. Before we start, let's look at one way to relax. Find a comfortable place to sit
or lie down or put your head on the desk. Close your eyes and slowly breathe in to
the count of 3 and out to the count of 3. Let's do this 5 times. The next time you feel
scared, angry or stressed, even if you can't close your eyes, try this. You will feel better
because your heartbeat will slow down and you can relax and think more clearly.

Help children understand that just as volcanoes explode when pressure builds up, people can also 'blow up' if they keep feelings inside and don't learn how to relax or share feelings with someone they trust. Harvard psychologist Harry Stack Sullivan spoke of children suffering in loneliness because of a developed 'delusion of uniqueness' (Siccone & Canfield, 1993, p. 137). In essence, they believe that they are the only ones facing burdens such as stress, fear of rejection or fighting parents. Teachers offer great support to children by helping them understand that everyone experiences negative emotions at some time, but the trick is to know how to manage them in socially acceptable ways.

At an early age children begin understanding the consequences of their emotional expression in different social contexts. Within the family they learn to repress or express emotions in healthy or unhealthy ways (Dunn et al., 1991) and they learn how their emotional behaviour affects others. Pressures at home, cultural and financial difficulties (Raver, 2004), parental expectations, the age and sometimes the gender of children all influence their ability to express and handle emotions. Many would agree that from an early age girls and boys continue to be socialised quite differently in regard to displaying and expressing emotions. Girls generally report feeling better after displaying and expressing emotions verbally, while boys tend to hide emotions more or express difficult emotions through mild aggressive or acting-out behaviour (Brody & Hall, 1993; Zeman & Shipman, 1996). 'Naughty' boys may be concealing personal and family issues and may need explicit teaching and reminding that while it is healthy to express emotions, this should be done in socially acceptable ways.

Children, particularly girls, learn quickly that expressing negative feelings is responded to less favourably than expressing positive emotions (Malatesta & Haviland, 1982). We often don't set girls up well. We can unconsciously reinforce the stereotype of good little girls, taking away their voice. Quiet girls are welcomed in busy classrooms and quiet isn't always healthy. We must consciously help girls to be more assertive and confident in expressing themselves, particularly those 'not so nice' emotions such as anger and frustration. Children learn the consequences of expressing emotions from the reaction they receive from others. They identify those who will support them and those from whom they believe it is wise to hide uncomfortable feelings (Zeman & Garber, 1996). Teachers who are approachable, warm and caring help children feel comfortable to reveal difficult emotions.

Fear and anxiety

It is never too early to talk openly to children about fears and other difficult feelings. Appropriate support for younger children can prevent fears and anxieties emerging as anger in older children (Vierhaus & Lohaus, 2009). Discussing fear provides an opportunity to reassure children and help them develop strategies to manage it. Children who handle problems alone are greatly disadvantaged because it is an exhausting exercise. Peer relationships, academic results and mental and physical health can all suffer.

Why are some children more vulnerable to fear and anxiety? Children who are over-protected by well-intentioned parents may begin to believe they cannot cope alone and are therefore more fearful. Some children's fears are the result of traumatic life experiences, such as fleeing from their country of origin as refugees or being part of communities affected by natural disasters like fire and flood. Powerful fears will need deep understanding by teachers and strong communication and partnership with parents who may also be traumatised. Referral to professional counselling and support may be required. Children can also suffer trauma when they vicariously experience violence and tragedy through seeing graphic media images. Younger children can be frightened by images of monsters and witches, while older children have increased fear and anxiety after watching news items involving violence and personal harm. Older children project themselves into these situations. Post-traumatic stress disorder, characterised by intense fear, helplessness and agitated behaviour at school, can be experienced by children up to two years after watching graphic and distressing media images (Wilson, 2008).

Common fears
Younger children fear being hurt, lost, left alone, getting into trouble, animals, spiders, strangers, darkness, catastrophic world events, not being

perfect or not being loved. Because of a fear of being hurt either physically or emotionally, teachers often see children *across all ages* unwilling to: use climbing or high play equipment; put their hand up to answer questions; join a group of peers; or to push themselves forwards to be part of a class presentation. Older children often worry unnecessarily that a particular situation will escalate and threaten their safety and security and that of loved ones. Great teachers work hard to step into the shoes of children and see the world through their eyes. Knowing children's major fears heightens teachers' sensitivity and helps them identify vulnerable children.

Children also have many fears and worries in relation to their home life, the effect of which inevitably spills over into the classroom. These include:

▶ parents separating, or illness and death of a parent. Because of cognitive egocentricity, children up to the age of 8 commonly see themselves as the primary cause of parents fighting or divorcing (Ablow et al., 2009)
▶ violence within the home
▶ mental illness, sickness or alcoholism within the family
▶ elderly family members needing extra care
▶ being replaced in the parents' affection by a new sibling
▶ financial worries or loss of employment
▶ moving house and losing friends.

As adults, it is easy to forget the devastating impact events and problems can have on children. In the midst of home upheavals and conflict, school may be the only stable factor in a child's life. Ideally, parents should inform schools about major changes or issues in a child's life so that teachers can be vigilant, patient and ready to offer appropriate support and reassurance (Peters Mayer, 2008). Because this is not always the case, teachers may need to take the initiative and gently approach parents in the hope of discovering what is upsetting these children. Teachers may also occasionally need to remind themselves that what can appear trivial to an adult can be very upsetting for children. The family dog may be sick!

Anxiety

Teachers can identify and make commonsense responses to the child who is frightened by the visiting dog or has a particular home issue, but it is more difficult to manage the constant, pervading sense of anxiety many children display. Concern should arise when anxiety interferes with children's daily activities and ability to be normal happy children. The debilitating effects of anxiety are outlined by Clark and Beck (2010, p. 51) who state:

> For the highly anxious individual worry takes on pathological features that do not lead to effective problem solving but rather to an escalation of the initial threat appraisal. Here the worry becomes uncontrollable and almost exclusively focused on negative, catastrophic, and threatening outcomes.

While many children and adolescents suffer from anxiety, girls of all ages report higher levels of anxiety than boys (King et al., 1989). Teachers must remember this because many girls successfully hide their fears and anxieties, which erodes their wellbeing. In children, shyness and anxiety are often related. Socially withdrawn children can be at risk for a range of negative outcomes, including socio-emotional difficulties (anxiety, low self-esteem, depressive symptoms and internalising problems), peer difficulties (rejection, victimisation, poor friendship quality) and school difficulties (poor teacher–child relationships, academic difficulties, school avoidance) (Rubin et al., 2009). Teachers help shy children enormously by identifying strategies to build their self-esteem and resilience (see Chapters 4 and 5) and by helping them to acquire the necessary social skills to mix more confidently with others (see Chapters 7, 8 and 9).

Transitional years of schooling can be filled with anxiety for many children. Entering their first year of formal schooling, moving up to a new class at the beginning of a year, changing school or starting secondary school can heighten children's stress and anxiety levels.

> At my son's school the approaching move into high [secondary] school was discussed in the classroom right through Year 6. Sometimes too much talk increases children's anxiety. My son became almost sick with worry. He was very sensitive about looking cool – actually not even cool – he just wanted to fit in with his peers and was terribly worried of somehow being embarrassed in front of them. The expression 'like a bear with a sore tooth' comes to mind. However, once he began attending high [secondary] school information and welcome evenings at the end of the year, he was a lot happier. That fear of the unknown had left him. I can remember thinking during my son's last year at primary school, 'I wish they would not make such a big deal out of it and just let the kids be!'
>
> **LOUISE, MOTHER OF RILEY, 13**

The transition to secondary school occurs at a time when children are traversing a very challenging developmental stage. They are leaving behind their familiar 'home' at primary school and entering the more demanding and adult-like setting of secondary school, as well as adjusting to the raging hormones of adolescence. This is when all of the social and emotional skills they have learnt in primary school will be called upon. To successfully handle this new world at secondary school they need to be independent, self-managing, confident, assertive, resilient, able to break into new social scenes and forge new friendships. The disparity in children's maturity and needs is most evident at these critical times of transition: starting primary school or moving to secondary school. Some children require enormous support, while others prefer a more casual approach. Parents and teachers walk a fine line between offering adequate reassurance and not increasing anxiety by putting too much focus on particular issues.

SIGNS OF ANXIETY

- Initially not wanting to leave parents or go to school
- Behaviour problems – easily angered, aggressiveness, hitting, biting
- Significant mood changes – irritability, frequent crying, sadness, lethargy
- Difficulty settling or hyperactivity
- Loss of appetite and weight loss, or gain in appetite and weight gain
- Frequent physical complaints
- Social withdrawal or school avoidance
- Declining academic results
- Excessive worry – catastrophic thinking (see Chapter 5)

Strategies to support fearful and anxious children

- Work through the questions in 'Evaluating Children's Social and Emotional Health' in Chapter 1 to gather information on a child's needs and vulnerabilities. What are the underlying issues causing the fear and anxiety?
- Safe and well-structured classrooms make children feel more secure.
- Pre-empt situations that may give rise to children's fear and anxiety by establishing safety nets such as: talking things through; Social Stories™ (see

Chapter 10); encouraging positive self-talk and rehearsal; modifying tasks; and setting achievable goals and timelines. These strategies all increase children's sense of security.

▶ Provide regular and positive feedback.

▶ Gradually help children overcome particular fears or anxieties by helping them step out of their comfort zone, baby step by baby step.

▶ Teach and reinforce optimism (see Chapter 5).

▶ Access teacher resources to support anxious children (see Attwood, 2004b). Strategies are equally valuable for all students.

▶ Role-play and picture storybooks are powerful avenues to help children explore and face fears and realise they are not alone in having particular fears.

▶ Display posters giving children practical strategies to handle stress and put-downs (see Chapter 5).

▶ Learning to relax is an art. Regular classroom relaxation sessions help all children, but particularly anxious children. Help children identify different ways to relax and list these on a classroom poster.

▶ Get a school dog! The therapeutic effect of animals is now well documented. There are many schools around the world 'employing' therapy dogs because of the happiness and invaluable calming and healing benefits they bring to all children, but especially to those who are anxious, shy, hyperactive, traumatised or suffering from an autism spectrum disorder or attention deficit hyperactivity disorder (ADHD). But don't forget to check the regulations applying to having animals in schools!

Murphy, our school's dog, is a Cavalier King Charles Spaniel Maltese cross. Two staff and I share his outside-hours care but Murphy belongs to everyone. We wanted a little dog so the kids could safely pick him up. He has a wonderful temperament and is very well behaved. His purpose is as a companion dog, but his role is really student welfare. He wanders in and out of classrooms, and if the kids are feeling a bit down, they know he'll always be up for a cuddle and that cheers them up. He sits in on music time and was even front and centre of our school photo. Murphy treats all children equally and, unlike other children and adults, does not judge them. He is 'someone' with unlimited love and time to make each child's day a better experience.

WAYNE ANDERSON, PRIMARY SCHOOL PRINCIPAL

Grief, loss and sadness

Younger children generally express grief, loss and sadness because of an inability to hide these feelings. However, a fear of appearing childish may prompt older children to suppress such feelings. The primary reason children of all ages openly express sadness is to receive emotional support (Zeman & Shipman, 1996) and it is imperative that teachers encourage children to do this. Internalising grief and attempting to handle it alone places children under enormous stress and can result in depression or anxiety. Times of grief and loss are particularly difficult when parents, other family members and friends are also grieving and struggling with disruptions and changes in their lives. Being surrounded by loved ones who are upset and 'off track' emotionally can be frightening and confusing for children. Their world can be changed in an instant, as indeed it can for the adults in their lives.

If parents are grieving or coping with a personal family crisis, they can't give as much to children as they normally would, and children can feel distanced and desperately vulnerable. Teachers can step in because children need adults they can talk to other than their parents. There's no 'normal' or obvious pattern to children's responses to trauma, although boys will generally become very aggressive, over-boisterous and demand attention, while girls tend to want to help. But the children who really need help are the ones teachers might not initially be aware of. Children to look out for, to really worry about, are those who are very quiet. Children also have a very low attention span when it comes to grief – that's their survival instinct kicking in. Their grief isn't always obvious. They may be playing and kicking a ball, yet feeling quite alone. Strong emotions often manifest themselves in physical symptoms including headaches, nausea, aches and pains. The ramifications of loss and trauma can seem relentless and inescapable to children – particularly when they are with grieving adults. Providing a stable link to the reality they once knew is where teachers come in. Children need routine, and classrooms can provide some much-needed semblance of normality. Teachers can help children represent their emotions in practical ways such as making masks of how they feel or making a stuffed toy and putting their feelings into it. Younger children can draw or paint their dreams. Teachers can also help students understand any involuntary, out of the ordinary behaviour, such as *nightmares and bedwetting, to help reduce feelings of self-consciousness and embarrassment.*

CATHERINE CINI, CHIEF EXECUTIVE OFFICER, GRIEFLINE

Children's understanding and concept of death varies significantly and experiences of grief and loss are expressed in many different ways, influenced by age, family and cultural background (Brent et al., 1996). Teachers must remember that in some cultures expressing grief openly is discouraged. Young children from all backgrounds often struggle to understand that death is permanent. We must remember that it is not until the age of 10 that most children understand the finality of death (Rosner et al., 2010). Sometimes children feel responsible for a death and cannot express their feelings in words. If the deceased person is a relative or family friend, they may begin worrying about the possible death of their parents or themselves ('Who will look after me?'). Older children have many of the same worries but begin to realise that death is permanent and are less likely to blame themselves. Bereaved children might show how deeply they have been affected by grief through uncharacteristic behaviour. This can include being angry, frustrated, tired and restless, acting out feelings rather than talking, changed eating patterns, reverting to younger behaviours such as sucking their thumb or lacking concentration and energy at school.

Children also experience deep loss and grief from other events apart from the death of a family member. Losses include:

▶ death of a pet
▶ separation or divorce of parents and subsequent separation from much-loved siblings or other close family members
▶ moving house, city or migration from another country
▶ dramatic changes in circumstances, such as loss of the family's financial stability
▶ a best friend leaving the school (this can have an enormous effect on a child, particularly if this is an only friend).

Strategies to help children handle grief, loss and sadness

▶ Find a private moment to gently tell children you are thinking of them at sad times. Let children know that you are always there for them to talk to when, and if, they feel like doing so. Acknowledging loss gives children permission to openly express sadness and accelerates the healing process.

▶ Many beautiful books are available to enrich sensitive class discussions and can help affected children gain empathy and support from classmates.

▶ Seek advice from school welfare staff and communicate with parents if a child appears unable to return to 'normal' after a reasonable period of time.

▶ Many schools have trained teacher facilitators to provide the Seasons for Growth program (Graham, 1997) that supports children through grief.

Attention seeking

Jimmy is a little boy in Year 2. He is bright and capable academically and quite personable one-to-one with the teacher. However, he will often burst into tears or start yelling over insignificant issues such as not having a pencil. He distracts others at his table so he is often moved and parents ask that their children are not seated next to him. His own mother is concerned that the teacher does not understand him and that the strategies being used to settle him to work are, in fact, punishing him. He will constantly call out, question the teacher, complain and say silly things to make the other children laugh. He isn't a bad kid, he just drives everyone nuts! He is an attention seeker!

PAUL, PRIMARY TEACHER

Most teachers will recognise this child. He is frustrating and exhausting ('Why does he act that way? What can I do? What am I doing wrong?'). All children want and need attention, but well-adjusted children don't crave inordinate amounts of it. No matter how much positive attention the 'Jimmys' receive, they demand more, even preferring negative attention to none at all. Parents and teachers dread the persistent pester-power of nagging children; the constant talker and interrupter, the grunter, wriggler, the comic and the crier. And sometimes many of these annoying habits are wrapped up in one little person.

Attention seeking can be the bane of a teacher's existence. Even one chronic attention seeker can wreak havoc on an otherwise great class, particularly if that student is popular with peers. To make matters worse, this behaviour can be contagious. Unless 'cured' by a skilled teacher, previously cooperative students can adopt the same behaviour. Many attention seekers are deeply unhappy and perceptive teachers see beyond the annoying and disruptive behaviour to discover underlying hurt, fears and hurdles in these children's lives. Often, even the smiles and jokes of class clowns are little more than cleverly applied disguises. Understanding why some children crave attention provides valuable insights into how to support them and reduce this challenging behaviour.

Sometimes attention-seeking behaviour occurs when children have a sense of entitlement that has developed as a result of parents giving in to their wishes. They often become defensive, blame their mistakes and misbehaviour on others and can develop a reputation for having a temper or become known as troublemakers. As people challenge them, they respond with angry outbursts of 'It's not fair!'. Ignoring attention-seeking behaviour can sometimes work, but it is not a long-term solution. While reassuring these children that they are valued and important members of the class, teachers can patiently explain how their behaviour adversely affects others. Teachers also need to ensure that boundaries are consistent and firm.

Other children crave attention at school because they don't get enough at home. They have an overriding need for affirmation (Grose, 2000). Some attention seekers hope to win or maintain acceptance from peers by becoming the class clown. Another group of attention seekers are those for whom school work is too easy or too difficult. Unless offered more challenging work, children who are very bright and find work boring can start exhibiting attention-seeking and negative behaviour (see Chapter 10). Those unable to cope with school work feel trapped and hide behind a facade of not taking work seriously.

Strategies to handle attention seekers

▶ Although easier said than done, rather than reacting to attention-seeking behaviour, a more effective strategy is to discover *why* and *when* children crave attention. Map behaviour patterns to reveal possible triggers and then look at ways to address these.

▶ Some attention seekers cease their annoying behaviour when they are allotted a special task. Catch them doing something right and praise them.

▶ After patiently explaining to children the negative effects of their behaviour on the class, teachers can negotiate behaviour-modifying goals, strategies to achieve these, checklists to help them self-monitor and rewards for improved behaviour.

▶ To pacify the chronic dobbers who have the same minor complaints after every recess, request that their complaints are placed into a suggestion box. Once a week, the teacher can discuss the complaints privately with these children and find solutions. This is cutting the nexus between the complaining and the constant attention they desire.

Impatience and impulsivity

Early childhood is often associated with young children's inability to control their impulses and emotions. Two-year-olds' tantrums in the supermarket and cries of 'Are we there yet?' are enough to have parents pulling their hair out! Entering their first year of formal schooling or Foundation class is a huge step for young children. Being allocated a Foundation class elicits strong emotions in staff; either they love the idea or are terrified. Every teacher knows that trying to corral these 'free range chooks' into an orderly class takes patience, consistency and the ability to endure ongoing nagging and dobbing (primarily from children, occasionally from their parents). Every Foundation teacher agrees, however, that at the end of the year they can look back with great satisfaction at the enormous progress in children's emotional and social growth. With teacher guidance and firm boundaries, children lacking some self-control in the Foundation Year generally mature and become more self-regulated as they move up the year levels. Unfortunately, some do not grow out of impulsive behaviour, and risk harming themselves and others as they charge into classrooms or vigorously swing across the monkey bars.

Children who are impulsive often make inappropriate comments, cannot control their emotions and act without considering others or being aware of the effects of their behaviour. These children may have trouble waiting their turn while playing a game or interrupt conversations and activities of others. This behaviour is disruptive, antisocial and alienates children from peers. When facing a problem-solving situation, they may respond quickly without thinking and make mistakes. In children, impulsivity is consistently associated with lower grades and achievement scores (Miyakawa, 2001). Some overly impulsive children may suffer from attention deficit hyperactivity disorder (ADHD) and will need specialist help (see Chapter 10). Impatient children can be just as trying for teachers as impulsive children, although not as dangerous to themselves or as annoying to others.

In a renowned study, called the marshmallow experiment, psychologist Walter Mischel observed a group of 4-year-olds (Shoda et al., 1990). Children were left alone with a marshmallow on the understanding that they could eat it immediately or wait a short time until the observer returned when they would receive two marshmallows. These children were tested again at 18 years old. Those who could delay eating the marshmallow at 4 years old, demonstrating control over gratification and impulses, had much higher college entrance scores than those who were impulsive. By adolescence, impulsive children are more likely to be stubborn, indecisive, easily upset by frustration, mistrustful, jealous and prone to fights and arguments (Goleman, 1997). A direct relationship has also been shown between the ability to self-control and the development of resilience (Eisenberg et al., 2004). Children able to control their behaviours have an advantage in adapting effectively to stressful situations and have more social competencies. Clearly, it is vital to help children acquire good self-regulatory ability as early as possible, certainly before they reach middle childhood and early adolescence where it facilitates the ability to form positive peer relationships.

Executive function is the working part of the brain that controls children's ability to plan, set goals, monitor progress, regulate attention and emotional responses to challenges and evaluate outcomes. Impulsive children often do not have good executive control, which affects both their academic and their social learning. Assisting children to articulate *how* they think about events (metacognition) and problem solve helps them change their thinking and behave more positively and less impulsively. Teachers can also help these children unpack their feelings and recognise what is causing their impulsive behaviour. Setting individual behaviour plans, with agreed strategies, goals and rewards, helps children learn to be more self-controlled and enjoy better relationships. Children can be guided to self-assess their behaviour and achievement, which increases their self-belief and self-regulatory ability (Zimmerman, 2000). Teachers could devise a series of hand signals to alert these children to their behaviour, and so trigger strategies for control.

Teaching children to master impatience and impulsivity involves teachers' time, persistence and endless patience, but children who can learn self-regulation will enjoy enhanced wellbeing.

PART THREE

Social development

seven

Social skills to build strong relationships

> Sam was not great at building social relationships. He enjoyed getting his own way and dominating play activities. Being big and loud, children reluctantly tolerated his behaviour but avoided him where possible. I worked hard to build a relationship with him by showing an interest in his great drawings. Finding an opportunity to speak to him privately, I finally put all cards on the table: 'Sam, I really like you, but other people don't have a chance to see the nice qualities I see. You know, if you listen to the other children, and take turns, they'll see the nice side of you too.'
>
> **TONY, PRIMARY SCHOOL, ASSISTANT PRINCIPAL**

People need people. The ability to build strong social relationships with people of all ages is a priceless life skill children need to enjoy school and to transition into a happy adolescence and adulthood. In partnership with parents, schools must help children acquire and refine this skill if they are to thrive in a world where teamwork and strong interpersonal skills are highly desirable. The next three chapters provide strategies to help children become more charming social animals. Strategies are also provided to involve parents in this important endeavour. Every important skill and attribute examined can be modelled by teachers, whose potential influence on young minds can never be overstated.

Empathy

Children who have empathy for others tend to be happier, more popular and do better in school because they generally get along well with others. Children lacking empathy have great difficulty making friends because they ignore the feelings of others (Webster-Stratton, 2002). However, as discussed in Chapter 3, children cannot appreciate how others feel until they understand their own feelings and this must be addressed in the early years. By the age of 4, children are developing the capacity to feel and express empathy. They can be encouraged to begin handling hypothetical questions such as, 'How would you feel if …?' By the age of 6 or 7 they are capable of walking in another's shoes (Caselman, 2007) and seeing the world through their eyes. At the age of 8, some children can grapple with more complex issues such as understanding that others may have feelings that differ from theirs. Empathy is learnt through experience and modelling, initially from parents and then reinforced by teachers and a school culture that values and cares for each school member.

We bought Tom pets to teach him empathy. As an only child he had no siblings to bang up against so we thought pets would help him learn to consider others smaller and more vulnerable than himself. When we bought a new kitten, we taught Tom (then 7) how to care for it by drawing a poster, which we put on the lounge room door. We wrote statements like 'Be kind and gentle' and 'Play nicely', then asked him to draw a picture of what he thought this looked like. We came up with six pictures of what the kitten would like, and wouldn't like, to remind him to consider the kitten's feelings. Now 12, Tom has a real love of animals and recently shouted across to kids chasing galahs on the school oval, 'That's not a nice way to treat birds.' Although shy, he makes friends because he is reasonable and tries to give and take in his friendships.

KIMBERLY, MOTHER OF TOM, 12

Strategies to help children develop empathy

▸ Discuss the importance and benefits of empathy, such as making friends more easily and getting along with people. Ask questions like: 'Can you think of a time when someone guessed you were sad or worried and spoke to you about this? How did you feel when this person showed empathy for you? Have you ever shown empathy for someone?'

▸ Photos of people in disadvantaged settings around the world can be the catalyst for powerful conversations about social justice issues and increase children's awareness of the way others live compared to their own lives. You can ask children questions such as, 'How do you think this little boy feels?' Students can share their reactions.

❱ Picture storybooks and movies help children step out of their familiar world and enter the reality of another person. Children can re-tell stories from the perspective of various characters.

❱ Using the writing component of literacy time, ask children to keep a journal for a week, pretending to be a completely different person; a disabled child or a famous actor. Visual learners may wish to illustrate their journals with drawings or pictures from magazines, while younger children can draw, or use colours and symbols. Praise children for portraying characters' feelings.

❱ Help children express empathy. Provide empathetic statements and questions for them to use such as, 'I'm sorry' or 'Can I do anything to help you?'

NEWSLETTER ITEM

How to help your child develop empathy

Children who develop and display empathy are happier and more successful at school and in life. Teachers help children to recognise, understand and show consideration for the feelings of others and parents can also contribute enormously to this important task. As opportunities arise – perhaps watching a TV program or discussing a news event – talk about how the people depicted might be feeling and encourage your children to express empathy for those in distress. For example: 'Wasn't Charlie brave … I'm sure Cathy must have felt very frightened … Has anything like this ever happened to you or your friends?'

Children often arrive home from school bursting with stories of the day's highlights and lowlights. Asking questions helps children empathise with others while gaining greater self-understanding: 'What happened before? What happened after? How did you feel? How do you think X was feeling? Why?' Praise your child for showing empathy. Parents are a child's first and most important teachers. When you model compassion and empathy, your child develops a greater ability to make and keep friends and relate to adults more confidently – parents and teachers included. It's a win-win!

Dave Riley and his colleagues, in a text written for early childhood educators, provide some excellent suggestions to promote children's emotional development. For example, perspective-taking can be encouraged by reading to children. Stories offer children safe settings in which to explore relationships. Discussing stories with children enhances their understanding. What might characters be feeling at different moments in the story? Parents and teachers can also help children explore how someone in the story could help a character to feel better.

A simple but important way to encourage compassion is for parents and teachers to notice when a child shares, takes turns or consoles another, and to reinforce such behaviour: 'I saw you give Molly a turn on your bike. That was kind. Then you were both able to have lots of fun.' Children do not always recognise when they are behaving in socially appropriate ways. Pointing this out and emphasising the positive consequences helps children become more aware of prosocial skills, appreciate their value and show accurate empathic responses.

DR TOM WHELAN, SENIOR LECTURER, SCHOOL OF PSYCHOLOGY, AUSTRALIAN CATHOLIC UNIVERSITY

Emotional intelligence

Children, particularly those in the higher levels, benefit from understanding that emotional intelligence (Goleman, 1996), which is the emotional equivalent of IQ, is now widely recognised as fundamentally important in all facets of life. This is empowering knowledge for children who are not high-flyers academically, but who possess other admirable and success-enhancing skills, such as interpersonal and intrapersonal skills. Academically gifted children must learn that results, unaccompanied by emotional intelligence, rarely bring happiness and success. Explaining and explicitly teaching emotional intelligence to children starts in the earliest years and its importance should be reinforced throughout their schooling. Emotional intelligence is:

- recognising and understanding your feelings and the feelings of others
- having empathy for others
- motivating yourself and others – even when things go wrong
- seeing things in a positive way.

Communication

Good communication is an invaluable social skill and teachers can help children master its building blocks. These include greeting skills, starting and holding a conversation, listening and showing interest, asking appropriate questions, using non-verbal language and body language, expressing an opinion, communicating feelings and reading the feelings of others (see Chapter 4). While some of these are sophisticated concepts, skilled teachers can help even the shyest children become better communicators. Literacy programs with a sound oral language component are vital given the close connection between a child's ability to express ideas and their overall happiness (Holder & Coleman, 2008). Articulate children have a marked head start in forming important relationships in and out of school. It is concerning that many children begin school unable to verbally communicate effectively, which, unless addressed, can hamper healthy social and emotional development.

> *Repeated research shows that about a fifth of children start school with weak verbal skills. Although the ability to communicate effectively is the key foundation to students' capacity to learn, speaking and listening skills have not been accorded the same significance as reading, writing, spelling and counting. Shortcomings in oral language can also have long-term effects on social behaviour, forming and maintaining friendships, self-confidence and identity. A key strategy to address this issue is to teach children to use 'self-talk'. It is a vehicle by which children manage and direct their thinking, what they do and how they make decisions, both about themselves, others and their world.*
>
> **ASSOCIATE PROFESSOR JOHN MUNRO, GRADUATE SCHOOL OF EDUCATION, UNIVERSITY OF MELBOURNE**

Children with receptive and expressive language disorders, attention deficit hyperactivity disorder (ADHD) or those within the autism spectrum will have greater difficulty communicating, and teachers should consult specialists in these areas to discuss how to offer appropriate support (see Chapter 10).

Strategies to help children develop better communication skills

▶ Explain to children the importance of communication skills in making friends and relating well to adults. Children must be explicitly taught to be sensitive to their audience so that they speak appropriately and ensure their listeners don't form inaccurate impressions.

▶ Through role-play, help children practise good communication in various social situations.

▶ Model good communication by teaching children the difference between hearing and active listening. Remind them to look at the speaker, nod, smile and show interest, and not look at the ground, yawn or fidget. You can ask children questions like: 'When someone really listens to you, how do you feel? Who is the best listener you know? Why? Are you a good listener?' Active listening helps children stop what they are doing, be quiet and listen while someone is speaking and absorb important information.

▶ Teach children responses that indicate they are listening and are interested: 'I see what you mean', 'Really' or 'That's interesting'.

▶ Help children master paraphrasing, which helps to avoid misunderstandings right through life. It is impressive and amusing to hear children demonstrate this powerful communication skill: 'I think you are saying that … Am I right?' Encourage children to ask questions when they are unsure of what is said.

▶ Children can develop good questioning skills through well-structured, rigorous adaptations of 'Show and Tell'. Set strict criteria for the length of talks, the depth of information to be delivered and the required volume, tone and pitch. Ask the audience to listen and prepare open-ended questions: 'How did you find your information? What did you most enjoy about your research?' Children should also practise giving compliments, which aids friendship-making: 'I really liked the way you arranged the text and pictures'.

▶ Public speaking and debating are useful ways to help children develop good communication and confidence. In upper levels, debating can become part of house competitions. Speaking at assemblies is an excellent learning experience but should be well-practised so that no child is left feeling foolish. Children who are shy or lack confidence need time with the teacher to discuss what they are going to say. Rehearsal and praise increases children's confidence and sets them up to succeed. Conversely, children who are 'out there' may need a private moment with the teacher to ensure that what they have planned to say is appropriate.

▶ Drama and acting classes strengthen children's communication skills, such as diction and pronunciation. Performing onstage teaches children to portray larger-than-life facial expressions and body language that can then simply be toned down and applied to other social situations, such as class presentations, meeting new people and even future job interviews.

▶ Display posters reminding children that learning to listen and show understanding is the cornerstone of good communication.

CLASSROOM POSTER

How to be a good listener:

▶ LOOK at the person speaking (this shows you care)
▶ LISTEN without interrupting and without getting distracted
▶ ASK questions to show you are interested
▶ NOD and make comments to show you understand
▶ REPEAT what you have heard in your own words ('Are you saying that … ?' or 'Do you mean that … ?')

▶ Display a poster outlining essential communication tips.

CLASSROOM POSTER

How to communicate confidently:

▶ STAND UP straight
▶ HEAD held high
▶ LOOK people in the eye
▶ SPEAK CLEARLY, but not too quickly.

Charm and manners

Children with high social and emotional intelligence generally possess both charm and manners, which shows respect for those around them. 'Manners and civilities are like "social oil" that helps relationships run smoothly' (Hromek, 2007, p. 8). It appears that increasing numbers of children (and young adults) have missed out on this vital information. Hearing a child spontaneously offer a 'Good morning' can pleasantly surprise many teachers. Some children are simply unaware of the positive impact simple social niceties can have on others. Explain that greetings such as 'Hello' or 'How are you?' require little effort, but reap enormous benefits. Those reaching middle and higher years without this knowledge are socially disadvantaged. Many children need guidance in giving compliments, respecting personal space, sharing, taking turns or responding when someone is sad. Learning not to interrupt and waiting until an adult has finished a phone call or speaking to another adult is also important. Children acquire charm and manners by observing those around them. Schools and classrooms need to set the standard. Teachers should model good manners and be persistent in demanding that good manners are exhibited at all times. Some children may need to be frequently reminded to demonstrate these attributes.

Many young children do not show basic manners, such as 'Please' and 'Thank you', which are so necessary in social interactions. There will be many times you need to tell them 'I don't have to put up with remarks like that' and walk away. Here are some strategies teachers and parents can use to help children acquire and remember to use basic manners:

1. *Demonstrate courtesy and use phrases like 'Thank you' and 'Excuse me'.*
2. *Kids learn from you so demonstrate kindness and compassion to others, such as asking people how they are.*
3. *Read books and watch movies that include core values you want children to learn.*
4. *Make requests of children and encourage them to be helpful.*
5. *Be prepared to be shocked when children are rude, and always remind them that this is not how we talk to people or behave.*

ANDREW FULLER, CLINICAL PSYCHOLOGIST

Strategies to help children develop charm and manners

▶ Innovative activities can teach children manners so that even those from the most disadvantaged or dysfunctional backgrounds have a smoother pathway into society. They are acquiring 'class' in class! Children can role-play various situations, such as 'Having lunch with the Prime Minister'. They can dress up, set the table, ask questions and respond appropriately as items are passed to them.

▶ Encourage children to write invitations to parents, other students or the principal to visit the classroom or view their work. Have a selection of special paper for them to write thank you notes to visitors.

▶ Include manners in classroom expectations because they are integral to showing respect for others.

▶ Introduce a weekly award for good manners.

Sense of humour

Children love to laugh. For them it is a natural and open way to view the world. A good laugh relieves tension and stress, elevates mood and provides an energy boost. Teachers and children work best when the atmosphere is light and playful and this also facilitates optimal social and emotional development. Children are drawn to others who are agreeable and fun to be with, particularly teachers who can laugh at their own mistakes. Children see these teachers as more 'human' and respect their honesty. Shared pleasure creates a sense of connection and a buffer against the stressful times of disagreement and disappointment. Laughter has healing properties. It is a particularly powerful antidote to depression and anxiety because laughter triggers the brain to release endorphins, which boost mood and diminish negative thoughts. Teachers may never know which children are in homes where, for a variety of reasons, there is not much laughter. Laughing at school may be the only time some children feel free to be a little carefree and silly if home is stressful.

Building a playful environment can therefore:

- strengthen student–teacher relationships
- assist in resolving disagreements
- relieve fatigue and energise children
- build students' resilience by helping them handle disappointments
- put things into perspective
- help children to relax.

However, teachers must also remember that some children use humour and playfulness to conceal hurt, anger and disappointment. Beware the 'class clowns'! Are they genuinely happy children or sometimes does the tone of voice, intensity or timing feel forced or not quite right?

Strategies to help children develop and appreciate humour

- Ask children to tell or listen to jokes. Compile a class joke book of limericks and knock-knock jokes. As part of the literacy program, organise a 'Bring-in-a-joke day' or ask children to write their own limericks. Children can also interview parents or grandparents and record their favourite jokes to share with the class. Children love hearing about funny experiences their parents and teachers had as children, particularly if they involve school.

▶ Compile a list of books children consider funny and show some funny YouTube videos of animals.

▶ Teach and model appropriate humour. Ask questions such as, 'Why do we laugh? When are jokes not funny? When can laughing be bad or wrong? What does it feel like when someone laughs *at* us?'

▶ Try replacing reprimands with humour. Rather than, 'Tuck that shirt in, please' or 'Please pull up those socks', use a humorous voice and feign shock or horror. You can often achieve more with a light-hearted approach than being heavy-handed. Remember … choose your battles!

Physical wellbeing

Healthy children are more alert, learn better and have greater energy to socialise and develop sound social and emotional skills. Regular physical activity is vital when we have rising levels of obesity in children (Ginsburg, 2007; see also Chapter 11). Today's decrease in children's physical activity is also linked to depression, attention deficit disorder (ADD) and stress (Brody, 2010). Regular physical activity reduces symptoms of depression with at least 60 minutes being recommended every day (VicHealth, 2011). However, children today are more sedentary than in previous generations due to the popularity of television, tablet computers, smart phones and electronic games. Since the 1970s, there has been a 25 per cent decrease in children's play time and a 50 per cent decrease in unstructured outdoor activities (Barros et al., 2009). Increasing children's outdoor play enhances fitness, improves critical-thinking skills, acts as a buffer against stressful life events and improves overall psychological wellbeing.

Clearly, teachers must encourage children to participate in sport and active play and teach them the benefits of regular exercise. Children are not making the most of lunchtime breaks to be active (Stanley et al., 2011). Many spend lunchtime sitting down, eating and talking. Although the social benefits of spending time with friends is important, children can still socialise with friends while engaging in physical activities. Schools should ensure that careful thought is put into playground design, with plentiful play equipment and appealing areas line-marked for games. Get them out there and give them something to do. More worrying is the fact that an even lower number of children are involved in physical activities after school.

Seeing and hearing difficulties

Within the learning context, observant teachers can be the first to notice children's hearing and eyesight difficulties. Parents may be unaware of these and their impact on children's academic progress and overall wellbeing. In some children, immature muscles behind the eye can cause difficulty with focussing or looking from the whiteboard to the page. Many young children in the early years also suffer from ear infections and upper respiratory conditions. Teachers, particularly in Foundation (first year of formal schooling) to Year 2, should monitor children's ability to hear as this can affect their ability to follow instructions or gain important foundational phonemic awareness. Early intervention is essential if academic, social and emotional development is not to be impeded. If young children fall behind academically, this can quickly affect their fragile self-esteem and make life unnecessarily difficult. These early years are when children are eager to please, easily hurt and anxiously seeking approval. Any concerns should be discussed with parents so that they can organise investigations with specialists, such as educational optometrists or audiologists.

Sleep

Sleep problems affect nearly a quarter of Australian children starting primary school. These problems are associated with poorer behaviour, social and emotional functioning, concentration and ability to learn. These are all things children need to achieve academically and to adjust to school. Having enough sleep each day may help children reach their potential during the important early years of their education.

JON QUACH, MURDOCH CHILDRENS RESEARCH INSTITUTE

Children aged 3 to 5 require at least 10 to 12 hours sleep, and those aged 6 to 12 require approximately 10 hours sleep (Iglowstein et al., 2003). When approaching puberty and going through growth spurts, children require even more sleep due to the massive physical and emotional growth occurring. Some parents are unaware of how important adequate sleep is in promoting children's good mental health (Chorney et al., 2008). Children who are frequently tired are unlikely to flourish at school. If teachers notice children falling asleep or being drowsy, they should speak with parents to identify any underlying issues.

Diet

A healthy diet gives children the energy to learn, play, make friends and thrive in the years when they are going through immense developmental changes. School canteens should provide healthy lunches. This supports teachers and parents as they encourage children to make healthy food choices. Dietitians view breakfast as an important meal to give children a good start to the day. If children are not being provided with breakfast at home, schools may need to be proactive in providing this, perhaps with donations from the local community. Observant teachers can detect children who are not eating an adequate amount of food from their lunch boxes. These children may be at risk of developing eating disorders (see Chapter 11) and parents need to be informed of extreme or atypical eating patterns. Children also stay more alert when encouraged to drink plenty of water for good hydration during the summer months or after physical education lessons.

Personal hygiene

Any teacher who has had to approach parents to ask for their cooperation in supporting a child whose smelly clothes, sneakers or body odour are offensive knows how hard this dreaded conversation can be. To minimise embarrassment, approach parents in a low-key and non-judgemental way as they are sometimes unaware of the problem. Ultimately, though, it is the child who suffers. Children who are different in any way are often ostracised or bullied. Basing a classroom learning activity around clean hands, fingernails, clothes and sneakers, as part of a healthy lifestyle, can be effective. As students move into that pre-pubescent stage, more frequent reminders about regular bathing and underarm deodorant may be required.

Strategies to become a health-promoting school

▶ Acknowledge that a healthy lifestyle is valued in the school community through articles in the school newsletter that focus on sports days and healthy eating.

▶ Have a sandwich or soup-making activity. Share healthy recipes and make a class recipe book.

▶ Provide an award for healthy lunches. Children can help create criteria for what are the healthiest items to include.

▶ Children love competition! Roster children to skip each day for 10 minutes, first thing in the morning or after lunch, and record the number of jumps to find the week's champion. Ensure there are plenty of ropes for lunchtime practice. Encourage older children to take aerobics sessions or ball games for the younger children at lunchtime.

▶ Invite sports people, nutritionists, doctors, dentists or nurses to speak about health and fitness. Consider approaching ex-students or parents.

▶ Make good use of the school's first aid person for talks on health and hygiene.

▶ There should be an expectation that every child participates in physical education lessons and sports events. Ensure activities are suitable for all skill levels.

▶ Brochures from local GPs, dentists, health care clinics/centres can be useful for classroom discussions on health and hygiene.

▶ For projects and group activities, investigate websites dedicated to healthy lifestyles that are suitable for children, and which provide great information and interactive games.

eight

Social skills to get along with others

Making friends

For teachers, the 80/20 rule can dominate playground duty: 80 per cent of the time dealing with friendship issues or spats and 20 per cent enjoying children's play or just chatting with them. Playground disputes and hurt feelings can then infiltrate classrooms where another 20 minutes is spent consoling, refereeing, arbitrating and finally getting students back on track. Piecing together the full story is imperative before that urgent phone call after school from a parent about her crying child and the unhappy experience with another one of *your* students!

For children, knowing how to develop and keep friendships can be the make-or-break factor in succeeding and being happy at school (see Chapter 3). Interestingly, this does not require them to be social butterflies. For children, what is important is not the quantity but the *quality* of peer relationships. Some children, particularly shy children, are content with one close friend and feel positive about school (Ladd, 1999). However, children who have a number of friends are generally more socially and emotionally savvy. They can empathise and play successfully, are friendly, positive and charming and are able to express themselves clearly and assertively. The role of online communication in making and sustaining friendships is a new and complex development and can be fraught with danger. Research clearly indicates that online communication can enhance the social connectedness, and even wellbeing, of young people when they communicate with existing friends. Early adolescents, particularly shyer boys, may benefit socially from instant messaging with friends and peers as this is easier than face-to-face communication. However, communication with cyber 'friends' who are in reality strangers, does not enhance social connectedness and wellbeing (Valkenburg & Peter, 2009). An over-reliance on cyber 'friends' does not give children the real human contact that everyone needs.

But what about children who have no friends? Teachers have a moral and professional responsibility to teach children friendship-making skills and to structure classrooms that facilitate making new friends and interacting successfully with peers. While more energy is spent helping younger children negotiate peer interactions, when friendships disintegrate in the older year levels the fallout can affect the whole class. Teaching children the rules and hidden secrets of the friendship 'game' eventually frees up precious time for the core business of teaching and results in happier and more responsive students.

It is easy to forget that things can look very different from a child's perspective. Adults look at the world through eyes that can see things, people and the connections between them as abstract relations, and can consider a range of possibilities. It is hard for adults to get back into the heads of children who only see the world in terms of the here and now. To help children develop strong interpersonal skills, it is important to stop, hold judgement and try seeing things from their perspective.

Research by Dodge and colleagues into aggressive children provides a useful approach to understanding children's friendships and social interactions. Each child has a 'database' of experiences, memories and social schemas. These form shifting lenses through which children process experience. Not everything about a situation is registered, but what is registered (or encoded) is rapidly given meaning (interpretation) that steers a child into certain courses of action. If my 'best friend' leaves me out of the group, I feel upset and before I know it, I am thinking that she meant to hurt me. Feeling upset and blaming my 'best friend' soon merges into thinking about how I can get back at her: 'Tomorrow I will invite the others to sit with me and ignore her.'

Adult observers can't always predict how children will interpret each other's behaviour; whether they will assume an intention to hurt, or attribute blame; what strategies they have at their command to handle hurt and disappointment in ways that will repair, damage or increase their chance of maintaining friendships. Sharpening our observation and listening skills, and remembering that children may see things differently to adults, opens the way for discussion and negotiation rather than blame and judgement.

MARY AINLEY, ASSOCIATE PROFESSOR, PSYCHOLOGICAL SCIENCES, UNIVERSITY OF MELBOURNE

Strategies to help children make friends

▶ Know children well and understand classroom dynamics, which are fundamental to helping them make new friends. Ask yourself: 'What's happening in this class?

▶ Gain greater control over classroom dynamics by using a sociogram, which is a graphic representation of interpersonal relationships in the classroom. Sociograms can reveal treasured alliances, hidden rifts, power cliques and children with few friends or connections. It is often surprising to discover who the influential students are. Ask children to write answers to questions. For example: 'Who are your three best friends in this group? Who would you like to be friends with? Which three children do you work with best? Who do you rarely play with?' Avoid negative questions ('Who *don't* you like?') as they can be confronting and uncomfortable for children striving to be compliant and tolerant. Children must know this information is confidential so that they are encouraged to be truthful. Information gained is useful when arranging seating and group activities, compiling groups for camps and organising class lists before transition to the next level. With this powerful knowledge, teachers can consciously structure groupings to diminish power bases, support healthy friendship groups and place shy children in groups where they will be welcomed and safe.

▶ Ask children to keep reflective journals and record feelings about schoolwork, goals, disappointments and friends. While being a powerful way for children to communicate with teachers in a safe and non-threatening way, teachers gain invaluable glimpses into the complicated world of children. Explain that journals will not be corrected, graded or shared with other students. If a journal entry reveals that a child is unhappy within their friendship group, make time to meet with this child to gently discuss this issue.

▶ Provide opportunities for children to discuss friendship issues through circle time. Children can discuss questions like: 'What makes a good friend? How can we make friends?'

▶ Through role-play, teach children the unspoken 'rules of the friendship game': not being too bossy or too self-absorbed to consider the opinions of others or too shy to walk up and ask to join an activity. Role-play helps children learn to read body language and social cues accurately (see information on Dodge's Model in Chapter 10, and body language in Chapter 4).

▶ Specialised care is needed for children with an autism spectrum disorder (ASD), including Asperger's syndrome. They will need intensive and explicit social skill teaching to help them make and keep friends.

Let's play

Play helps children acquire and polish social skills, such as how to enter a group, abide by the rules, be fair, honest and imaginative, make decisions, display leadership, problem solve, negotiate, compromise and share. This is when children really learn to understand another's perspective and feelings, because they have to get along for the game to continue. If conflict escalates, teacher intervention is necessary, but teachers should not be tempted to jump in too soon. As with all social skills, practice makes perfect. Play contributes to the cognitive, physical, social and emotional wellbeing of children and, importantly, helps them manage stress and become more resilient (Ginsburg, 2007).

Psychologists have long-recognised the value of play and make-believe for children. 'In play a child always behaves beyond his average age … it is as though he is a head taller than himself' (Vygotsky, 1978, p. 102). While acting out real-life scenarios, children take on various roles and develop the ability to control feelings and impulses. They discover interests, learn to explore and master new obstacles without fear of failing. All of this can lead to greater self-confidence. Active play also improves children's fitness and helps to reduce obesity levels (Burdette & Whitaker, 2005). Teachers learn volumes about children and their social and emotional development through observing them at play.

Child-directed play should remain a sacrosanct part of childhood. Children need space to unwind and simply have fun. Experts are greatly concerned at the reduction in playtime occurring in many United States preschools and primary schools to allow greater time for academic pursuits (Ginsburg, 2007). Ironically, studies show that students are less fidgety and more attentive after recess resulting in better classroom behaviour and better learning (Barros et al., 2009; Pellegrini, 2009). Most teachers would agree that all children, but particularly boys, benefit from playtime activity that allows them to unwind and let off steam. Although there has not been an official reduction in playtime in Australian schools, the ever-growing emphasis on improving standards in literacy and numeracy has resulted in an increased pace and intensity within the classroom. This makes playtime more precious than ever before (for children and teachers).

Many children come to school looking forward to playtime as the most important time in their day, while others dread it. The unstructured nature of the playground means that it has the potential to be disastrous for the socially and emotionally unskilled child. This is where bullying and exclusion mainly occur, scarring children for life. It is a different experience for the socially-adept child who is 'king-of-the-kids' and happily tears around with a mob of friends. Observant teachers notice children who don't mix with peers at recess or lunchtime, but take sanctuary in the library or sit alone. Certain children sometimes prefer their own company. However, if this becomes their normal practice, teachers may need to intervene and provide strategies to help these children make friends.

Handling conflict constructively

Children must be able to settle differences positively and assertively if they are to successfully interact with others. They also need frequent reminders that saying sorry is a sign of strength, not weakness. Many excellent resources, such as *Cool calm kids* (Suckling & Temple, 2008), provide classroom activities that can empower children to handle conflict effectively. Sometimes children also need help recovering from conflict situations. For example, Sally tells you that she is upset to be in the same class as Rita because Rita has been mean to her. Asking for details about what happened can be very revealing: 'She picked on me … in Year 2' (Sally is now in Year 4!). Although this can be amusing for adults, for Sally the hurt is still very real even two years later. Clearly, Sally must learn to forgive and move on, but the discussion and approach should be handled sensitively. Situations of conflict among children or between teachers and children can be valuable teaching moments that develop children's social skills (Dunn, 1988). Many teachers will recall times when they successfully used situations of conflict in the classroom or schoolyard to teach children vital lessons.

Strategies to help children handle conflict constructively

▶ Teach children the words 'assertive', 'passive' and 'aggressive' and brainstorm examples. With practice, all children can learn to be assertive, which increases self-confidence and helps them resist peer pressure.

▶ Introduce children to 'I' statements. Explain that even adults use these to express feelings without hurting, angering or attacking others. For example: 'I don't like it when you speak to me like that. I feel upset when you shout'.

▶ Teach children how to resolve disagreements. For example: 'How can disagreements be handled so that everyone is happy? What does the word "compromise" mean?' Display a poster reminding children about strategies to resolve conflicts and review these regularly.

CLASSROOM POSTER

How to resolve conflicts:

▶ STOP! Don't let the conflict get worse.
▶ SAY what the conflict is about. What does each person want or not want?
▶ THINK of positive options to be fair to everyone.
▶ CHOOSE a positive option each person can agree on.
▶ ASK someone for advice if you can't agree.

Rules:

▶ Agree to fix the problem.
▶ Don't use put-downs.
▶ Take turns talking. Don't interrupt.
▶ Be clear and honest about how you feel.
▶ Listen to how the other person feels.
▶ If you still don't understand, ask more questions.
▶ Use your head. Don't act out!
▶ Be prepared to compromise.

Teamwork

Teamwork is a difficult concept for children, especially the younger ones. Putting aside one's own opinions and compromising for the good of the group is hard even for adults. Many children have difficulty sharing and working with others on a project and need help and explicit teaching to acquire these important skills. Joining a sports team or being part of the student representative council or drama production help children learn teamwork skills. Cooperative learning strategies are another powerful tool for classroom teachers to use in helping children to develop teamwork skills.

In over 30 years of teaching, I've never seen any teaching practice enthuse students and teachers more than cooperative learning (CL). CL redefines student engagement in an authentic, sustainable and exciting way. Properly implemented, it simultaneously improves children's academic performance and social development and is appropriate to all year levels and content areas. My teachers quickly noticed a positive change in students' attitude to school and a measurable improvement in learning. One of the most dramatic developments relating to our introduction of CL has been its impact on a 9-year-old suffering from selective mutism. Cooperative learning's key elements of positive interdependence and mutually supportive interaction provided this student with a genuinely non-threatening environment in which to participate in classroom activities at a level well above expectations.

At the very beginning of our training, teachers realised that group work is not cooperative learning. There's nothing particularly clever about having students work in pairs or small groups where some compete with team mates, others work independently or freeload and contribute nothing. To structure CL effectively, teachers must ensure all key elements are present and this requires higher-order professional knowledge and practice.

JOSEPH KELLY, PRIMARY PRINCIPAL

Cooperative learning promotes children's engagement and motivation because it requires listening to others and communicating in deep and meaningful ways, taking personal responsibility for a task, managing conflict and trusting group members. Children can carry these teamwork skills into their senior school years and adult lives where the ability to work cooperatively is an invaluable career and life skill. Moreover, self-worth is enhanced because each child's contribution is important and integral to the group's success.

Strategies to help children develop teamwork skills

▶ No matter what the team is, sporting or academic, teachers must set strong goals, criteria for reaching those goals and clearly defined roles for each group member. Teachers need to guide children to self-monitor, pull their weight, support each other and stay on task so that conflict is avoided. Orchestrate opportunities for all students to experience leadership.

▶ Teachers can utilise the existing house system to build team spirit. In addition to forging an emotional connection and loyalty to their house, all children can play an important role that contributes to the success of the group.

Winning, losing and moving on

Much of what goes on at school will, for some children and their parents, have a competitive edge to it. Healthy competition helps raise the bar for children's performance and is simply part of life and part of building resilience. Winning and success build children's self-esteem but children also learn a valuable lesson when they taste and accept failure and get back up and try again (see Chapter 5). Teachers should encourage children to value trying. Nobody wins all of the time. When children are over-protected and sheltered from the realities of life, we do them a disservice. They will lack the inner strength (resilience) that protects them from developing anxiety and depression, particularly in later, more vulnerable years.

Some parents will complain that lack of competition breeds mediocrity and there is an element of truth in this. But teachers must resist allowing competition in class to spiral out of control. Minimising comparison with peers protects the self-esteem of those children who will never be the fastest and those who find competition stressful. The personal-best approach encourages children to compete against themselves, striving for continual improvement rather than competing against others.

Accepting rules, authority and relating to adults

Most children generally follow classroom and school rules and are anxious to please, particularly in the early years. From the age of 10 or 11, however, rules can be harder to enforce as children struggle to refine their identity and display their independence. How a child accepts rules and authority and relates to adults depends greatly on how these attitudes are fostered at home. Undoubtedly, home values flow into children's school life and it is difficult for teachers to gain respect if little is shown for teachers or authority at home.

Children are more likely to accept school or class rules and the teacher's authority when there is a strong teacher–student relationship based on mutual respect and trust. Traditionally, children complain about 'tough' law-enforcing teachers. However, these can be the very teachers children admire most, particularly when high standards are upheld with fairness and consistency. Children also learn social responsibility through understanding they can't always have their own way in life, especially if this is detrimental to the good of the group. They are learning that choices and decisions have social and emotional consequences for themselves and others.

In today's media-saturated world, experts increasingly see a link between children's exposure to violence and their unwillingness to behave in a socially acceptable way.

Children are adopting the anti-social behaviour of much older children with psychologists seeing children as young as 5 being suspended from school. Tacit acceptance of early exposure to violence on TV and the internet is part of the 'downward creep' of bad behaviour from older teenagers to much younger children. Rather than passively accepting violence as a legitimate form of children's 'entertainment', we must stop and think long and hard about how we glamorise and normalise violence in many areas of life, such as sport and the media, and especially how we allow our children open-slather access to violent video games and internet material.

SIMON CRISP, PSYCHOLOGIST

Strategies to help children accept rules, authority and relate to adults

- At the beginning of every year, set classroom expectations and rules through whole-class negotiation. Owning the rules and consequences of infringements is the first step to ensuring that children accept them as fair and appropriate.
- Discuss rules in the wider society asking children to consider why they were made and who they protect.

▶ If an individual child is not showing a willingness to follow rules and be respectful, it is important that someone the child respects sits down and takes the time to unpack what is going on, and what the child may see as the issue. Happy children want to fit in, and emotionally have a *need* to fit in. The challenge is to identify what is causing children to be so unhappy and angry that they insist on 'bumping up' against authority and classroom norms.

Social skills to build inner strength

Independence, responsibility, problem solving, decision making and a sense of right and wrong are essential qualities and skills that can be fostered with ongoing support as children mature. More than ever before, these are needed to navigate today's complex and challenging world.

Independence

The ability to function independently underpins children's successful social and emotional development and certainly their academic progress. It is an important emotional task for children to achieve in the early years and becomes even more important in the upper levels of primary school. However, there is growing evidence that parental anxiety over children's safety is impeding their ability to develop independence (Sutterby, 2009). Over-controlling and over-protective parenting restricts children's behaviour, discourages healthy opportunities for independence and can result in children becoming anxious and socially withdrawn (Rubin et al., 2009). As children enter school for the first time, some parents are reluctant to loosen the apron strings. It's often the parents who are crying, not the children.

Right from their first year of school, children want to show how grown up they are. They love showing their independence even in small ways or through small tasks. By the age of 8 or 9, it is normal and healthy for children to want greater independence. As children grow older, they are disadvantaged if they cannot work independently without constant reassurance or reminders to stay focused. Children who are given some independence at home will display more independence at school. Those who cannot function independently and confidently before reaching secondary school will certainly be disadvantaged academically and will stand out as socially and emotionally immature among their peers. School newsletters can encourage parents to give children age-appropriate tasks to develop independence, which also increase self-confidence and self-esteem. Where possible, children around the age of 10 should be encouraged to use public transport or walk independently to and from school. Often children can arrange to walk with siblings or friends living nearby. Independent mobility is a significant milestone for children. As Zubrick et al. (2010, p. 8) state:

> *Children have a greater opportunity to interact with other children when they are not under adult supervision. This fosters independence and responsibility, which in turn builds children's confidence and social skills.*

Strategies to help children develop independence

▶ Children who frequently seek teacher affirmation should be led to trust themselves and work more autonomously over time. A child may initially want teacher feedback every five minutes, but this over-dependence can be progressively reduced through negotiating small goals, which include extending the time between each contact with the teacher.

▶ Parents need to be informed of any classroom strategies so they understand the work of teachers to develop their child's independence. They should support the effort of teachers by expecting children to pack their school bag, carry it into school and remember their sports gear and homework. It's the small things that make the difference. Parents can also be guided to set other achievable tasks so that children are not overwhelmed (Brown, 2009), but develop greater independence through stepping outside their comfort zones.

Responsibility

Children as young as 3 and 4 yearn to prove they can undertake new tasks. Gaining a sense of responsibility is an integral part of healthy social and emotional development and is seen as a sign of growing up by both children themselves and those around them. We've all been dazzled by the glowing face of a child who proudly says, 'Look what I've done. I put my toys away all by myself.' We teach responsibility by giving it and helping children learn to be accountable for their actions (Grose, 2000). Children whose parents have allowed them to test their wings and take on responsibility in a supportive and warm setting can take responsibility for themselves and their actions at school. Those not so lucky will hang back and avoid, or even refuse to accept, new responsibilities. They have had too much done for them and have never had the opportunity to develop a sense of responsibility.

In most classes, children will have had discussions about rights and responsibilities as part of forming classroom norms. This is a wonderful opportunity to build their understanding of the importance of responsibility. If children are given the right to take classroom balls and skipping ropes out at playtime, they are responsible for bringing them back. This is an important lesson for children to learn. Children who are irresponsible and who cannot be relied upon will find it more difficult to make and keep friends, particularly as they grow older and peer acceptance becomes paramount.

Strategies to help children develop responsibility

▶ Explicitly outline expectations so that children have a clear idea of their responsibilities to themselves, to each other and to the school.

▶ 'Target' children afraid of responsibility and those who need to develop the ability to act responsibly. Find them opportunities to undertake new responsibilities and praise their achievements: 'John, I have a very important job for you. Could you please collect our books from the librarian? I know I can rely on you.'

▶ Ask children to interview their parents or another relative such as a grandparent. They could ask questions such as, 'When you were my age, what responsibilities did you have at home and at school?' Now ask children to list and compare their responsibilities with those of the person they have interviewed.

NEWSLETTER ITEM

How to help your child develop greater responsibility

Some children adore increased responsibility, others shy away. Children who are given opportunities to be responsible for themselves and for particular tasks gain greater self-confidence and relate more positively to others. At school we encourage children to take responsibility for their possessions, school property and their words, actions and relationships with others. We know that children will not always succeed or remember their responsibilities; however, all children improve over time, particularly with our continued display of confidence in them and gentle, but firm, reminders. Parents have many wonderful opportunities to help children learn to accept and handle responsibilities. Children can take responsibility for cleaning their room, for putting personal possessions away and for feeding family pets. They can also be given a 'chore' that helps the smooth running of the family day, such as drying the dishes, setting the table or putting out the cereal and milk each morning. Negotiate an achievable responsibility with your child and make it clear that this is an important duty and you are confident it will be completed well. Regardless of how busy your child is with school work or extracurricular activities, every child learns to appreciate others more and to have greater self-pride when given responsibilities around the home. Children who can accept responsibility generally do better at school and have the confidence to tackle new tasks.

Problem solving, decision making and accepting consequences

Children who can effectively solve problems are more cooperative both at school and at home. Their improved conflict-resolution ability makes them more popular with peers (Webster-Stratton, 2002). The ability to effectively solve their problems helps children handle anger, conflict and difficult social situations. They also have greater protection against depression (Spence et al., 2005). Children who are good problem-solvers can identify a greater range of positive solutions to problems providing them with confidence and a sense of control over difficult situations. All of this underpins healthy social and emotional development.

Strategies to help children solve problems, make decisions and accept consequences

▶ Children can learn to solve problems and make better decisions through classroom discussions that brainstorm multiple solutions to common problems and the consequences of these solutions. This assists the many children who have difficulty thinking ahead to the consequences of their decisions.

▶ Teachers are familiar with Y-charts, mind mapping and fishbone diagrams. Children can use these graphic organisers as templates to record steps to solve everyday problems. Strategies for solving mathematical problems, such as drawing a model, working backwards, acting it out or doing a simpler problem, can also be applied to solving everyday problems. Being able to transfer explicitly taught mathematical problem solving and decision making to solve any problem can be a handy tool for children.

▶ Promoting the role of the student representative council is an effective way to help children see problem solving and decision making in action.

▶ Problem solving can be explicitly taught to children through clear and logical steps. These can be displayed on classroom posters.

CLASSROOM POSTER

How to be a great problem-solver:

▶ IDENTIFY the problem
▶ WHY is this happening?
▶ LIST some solutions (discuss these with someone)
▶ CHOOSE the best solution
▶ TRY it!
▶ EVALUATE your choice (How did it work? Would you do this again? What did you learn?).

Sense of right and wrong

From ages 4 to 5, children begin grasping the concept of right and wrong, good and bad and the infamous 'That's not fair!' emerges (Brazelton & Sparrow, 2005). Before the age of 6, children have difficulty distinguishing fantasy from reality and it is not unusual for them to make up stories, occasionally fib or cheat, deny actions or blame others for their mistakes. They simply need the adults in their world to gently, but firmly, remind them of the right thing to do without unduly embarrassing them and damaging their self-esteem. However, children who continue to lie, particularly after the age of 6, may have underlying emotional problems affecting their moral development and require professional counselling.

From age 5 or 6, children also begin noticing differences between themselves and others. Teasing often occurs unless children are guided by parents and teachers to acknowledge that, yes, we are not all the same and that's okay. By modelling acceptance of difference, teachers help children understand that a sense of right and wrong involves far more than simply telling the truth or not stealing. Children must start understanding that teasing, bullying, exclusion and peer pressure to conform are as unacceptable as dishonesty. From age 7 onwards, children can discuss increasingly complex moral issues and are capable of walking in another's shoes. Teachers and parents will notice with concealed amusement that 8- and 9-year-olds often passionately adopt a particular cause, be that climate change or protecting the habitat of the hairy-nosed wombat. Working out what they value and believe in is an important emotional task for children, and their feelings about adopted causes should be affirmed and praised.

From age 10 or 11, most children will have developed a strong sense of justice. Yet, just around the corner is the time when they are increasingly tempted to bend rules to impress friends. This occurs as they speed toward adolescence where rules and boundaries are invariably challenged as part of the forging of independence and identity. However, if from the early years children have received strong moral guidance and the opportunity to participate in rigorous discussions of moral issues, their rule-breaking will be annoying and frustrating rather than a source of serious concern.

Kohlberg's six stages of moral development are still revered today and contain some salient messages for teachers. In Kohlberg's theory, individuals advance to higher moral stages as they are increasingly motivated to act from a belief in the importance of doing the right thing rather than merely to avoid punishment or criticism. Blatt and Kohlberg (1975) studied the effects of discussing moral issues with children using a Socratic method of teaching. In this approach, children learn to freely express opinions. Teachers ask children questions that prompt them to re-evaluate those opinions while considering and respecting the opinions of others. Importantly, children were presented with arguments and moral dilemmas one stage above that of most children at their age. This successfully challenged and stimulated them to think more deeply and form more complex views. The significance of this for teachers is clear. Engaging children in meaningful and challenging discussions prompts them to think before acting and to develop a higher level of morality.

Why is moral development important in the social and emotional development of children? Children lacking a morality similar to that of their peers are viewed negatively and have greater difficulty establishing friendships. What is forgivable in the first year of school isn't accepted by peers or teachers four or five years later. While children need guidance in establishing a moral compass, they also benefit from knowing they will be forgiven if they make a mistake. Those who experience real forgiveness learn more quickly to be honest and to accept responsibility for their words and actions. Responding to this, most schools have adopted a restorative justice approach to unacceptable behaviour rather than punitive responses (Morrison, 2002). Restorative justice ensures that negative behaviour is not condoned, and children who hurt others must confront their misdemeanours and their victims. However, they are supported, respected and given an opportunity to rebuild their social relationships and to become positive and resilient members of that community. When admired adults (parents and teachers) are willing to say 'sorry', children also learn another powerful moral lesson.

> *We discovered that Chloe, a Year 6 student, had stolen two books from the book fair. I contacted her mother who was very supportive, and invited her to a meeting that afternoon. Chloe, a hard worker and a happy child, said she had wanted to buy a book for her little brother who was home sick but she didn't have enough money. It was clear that Chloe's desire to buy something for her brother had clouded her judgement and she had made an impulsive, but poor, choice. At the meeting, Chloe cried and expressed great regret for her actions. Mum was teary too. While I made it clear that what Chloe had done was wrong, I also said she could move forward and show us that she had learnt a valuable lesson. She left that room knowing that she had a second chance. Over the rest of the year she certainly proved that she was a valued and strong member of the school. Sometimes good children simply make wrong decisions and deserve a chance to redeem themselves.*
>
> **HELEN, PRIMARY SCHOOL PRINCIPAL**

Harvard psychology lecturer Richard Weissbourd (2009) has identified parenting practices that unintentionally undermine the moral development of children. Many parents focus too intensely on their children's happiness

and achievements while neglecting to cultivate their morality to the same degree. Weissbourd's research (2011) found that two-thirds of children interviewed considered happiness more important than being a good person and caring about others. Children also believe it is more important to their parents that they are happy rather than good. These are worrying beliefs for children's moral development.

There also appears to be a rapidly diminishing presence of 'old fashioned' values in today's secular and materialistic society. If children do not have strong modelling in ethical thinking and behaviour from their parents and teachers, then they will gain their values and moral reasoning from the media, which can normalise violence, lack of care for others and a 'me-first' attitude. Parents and teachers must actively help children formulate a moral code to live by so that they make safe and responsible decisions and are caring, sensitive and happier members of society.

Strategies to help children develop a sense of right and wrong

▶ Model respect for honesty, rules and the rights of others, and praise children for behaving ethically. The playground is where children practise these important social behaviours and teachers on playground duty need to be watchful and supportive of this learning. Turning a blind eye to children breaking the rules, being aggressive or speaking unkindly to others undoes all of the hard work undertaken through classroom activities.

▶ Engage children, particularly those with behaviour issues, in supportive and Socratic discussions of real-life situations. Lecturing and berating children leads to defensiveness rather than more moral and socially acceptable behaviour (Walker et al., 2000).

▶ Because peers can be more influential in children's moral development than parents (Walker et al., 2000), provide opportunities for children with a highly developed sense of morality to become leaders and role models for other students.

▶ Ask children to write funny stories about characters that lie, and then feel compelled to invent many more lies to conceal the truth (the boy who cried 'wolf').

▶ Guide children to want to do the right thing for the right reason by involving them in the establishment and ownership of classroom expectations, based on honesty, respect and care for all.

PART FOUR

Sleepless-night issues

ten

Facing the tough stuff head-on

Bullies and victims

> I was bullied by most of the boys because I played with girls. I was called a girl, I felt unsafe and threatened. They were sometimes physical. I'd hide in the toilet cubicle to stay safe. Getting bullied made me feel like committing suicide. In my journal I wrote down ways to do it; jump out of a moving car, stab myself with a sharp knife from the kitchen, run away at night and hope someone would kill me. Getting bullied made me wonder why I was born. I didn't tell Mum and Dad because I thought they couldn't do anything. I told them in late Year 2 because I kept coming home crying and Mum always asked what's wrong. I didn't tell the teachers because bullies are sneaky. They go up first and say something untrue about you. Teachers believe the person who approaches them first. To the teachers, I'd say to LISTEN and consider BOTH sides of the problem. Talk to the whole class about being nice to everyone. My Year 3 teacher was by far the most helpful. She always listened carefully and always suggested good things like putting my pencil case on her desk to show her I needed to talk. Also my principal was by my side. He said I could just walk into his office to talk. I felt safer because I had help and support.
>
> JOHN, 11

Bullying can wreck havoc with children's social and emotional development and their ability to be happy and successful at school and even long into the future. How can children complete essential social and emotional tasks, such as managing emotions, establishing friendships and forming a healthy self-esteem, if every moment is overshadowed by the faces of bullies, or the shame of witnessing bullying and being too afraid to act? Teachers must be very familiar with every aspect of bullying if they are to prevent long-lasting damage to children's socio-emotional wellbeing.

Bullying is an age-old occurrence as evidenced in stories from parents and grandparents, yet only recently has the long-lasting damage of bullying been recognised. Scandinavian professor Dan Olweus (1978) was one of the first to recognise the devastating damage bullying inflicts. Today we know that over 70 per cent of schoolchildren have been victims of bullying (Peters Mayer, 2008) with 25 per cent being bullied daily (Eisen & Engler, 2007). Constant images of schoolyard bullying in the media, YouTube, Facebook and the internet have certainly changed perceptions that bullying is a normal part of school life and, thankfully, the 'grin and bear it' mentality is now unacceptable.

Many parents are lost and panic-stricken when confronted with their child being bullied. Most teachers would have experienced at least one irate, stressed or tearful parent communicating by email or arriving at their door to demand action to support their bullied child. This is a challenging situation, particularly if teachers are unaware of the bullying, or the alleged bully appears to be a diligent and compliant child in the classroom. Moreover, sometimes the behaviour of the alleged victim brings their innocence into question. Teachers can feel powerless if unable to answer searching questions from a mother who tells them that her child is reluctant to come to school, cries at night and is not eating. She is fed up with the situation and intends approaching a higher authority; the Principal and possibly the media! As parents often lay the full weight of solving the problem on the teacher's shoulders for a *quick* solution, this is indeed a sleepless-night issue. While teachers often believe they can identify bullying, research indicates they sometimes overestimate their ability to detect it (Yoon & Kerber, 2003). Every teacher should be very familiar with the signs that a child may be a victim of bullying and be aware of its devastating effects.

SIGNS OF BULLYING

> ▸ *Emotional* – crying, moodiness, negativity, depression, unexplained anxiety, swearing, sadness, anger and aggression, refusing to talk about what is wrong, thoughts of self-harm and suicidal ideation (children's drawings can reveal emotional distress)

▶ *Social* – withdrawing from activities and becoming isolated, spending most breaks in the school library, reluctance to walk to or from school and bullying other children

▶ *Physical* – tiredness, unexplained bruises and cuts, appetite changes, frequently claiming illness and damaged or 'lost' property

▶ *Academic* – school refusal, declining results and interest in school

LONG-TERM EFFECTS OF BULLYING

▶ Lingering feelings of anger and bitterness leading to a desire for revenge
▶ Difficulty trusting people
▶ An increased tendency to be a loner
▶ Low self-esteem
▶ Long-term reduced occupational opportunities

Bullying is a negative action that is repeated over time, and victims often have difficulty defending themselves from perpetrators. It may involve physical contact, words, making faces or negative gestures or refusing to comply with another person's wishes. It can be difficult to detect as many bullies are skilled actors employing tactics including indirect bullying, exclusion, nasty jokes to humiliate or embarrass, mimicking and spreading rumours and/or lies. While both boys and girls inflict verbal, physical and psychological bullying, boys use more physical, rough-and-tumble aggression often resulting in externalised retaliation, such as fighting back (Field, 2007). The physical nature of boys' bullying makes it easier to detect than girls' skilfully camouflaged bullying, leading to the misconception that boys bully more than girls (Beane, 2008). Girls' bullying is more relational, covert and inflicts psychological pain through rumour-spreading, exclusion, snide remarks and negative body language (Field, 2007; Olweus, 1993; Simmons, 2002). Frighteningly, girls are becoming more physical in their bullying (Beane, 2008). *Odd girl out* (Simmons, 2002) highlights the complexities of girls' bullying behaviour. Many victims of bullying become bullies themselves to find acceptance and stop the bullying they are experiencing (Peters Mayer, 2008).

Cyberbullying is an insidious means of inflicting harm via the ever-increasing variety of information and communication technologies young people adore. Sixty-two per cent of primary teachers report cyberbullying as being a problem, with 5 per cent indicating major issues (Galaxy Research, 2011). Teachers need to know that cyberbullying victims suffer *higher* levels of depression than victims of all other forms of bullying (Wang et al., 2011). Faceless cyberbullies wield the frightening power to instantly disseminate damaging and often false information to millions, leaving victims feeling isolated, helpless and dehumanised. This can cause devastating damage to emotionally vulnerable children whose resilience, self-esteem and identity are fragile and still being formed.

Teachers address bullying more effectively when their beliefs and attitudes to bullying are carefully considered and well-informed by research. Troop-Gordon and Quenette (2010) found that children view teachers as responding to bullying in two main ways. Teachers who engage in *active* intervention, such as reprimanding bullies, separating students or contacting parents, are viewed by children as empathetic. Therefore, victimised children feel accepted and not guilty about being bullied, and are more protected from the damage bullying causes. However, teachers who engage in *passive* intervention, such as advising victims to avoid bullies or to stand up for themselves, make victims feel inadequate and somehow responsible for being bullied. These children believe teachers are indifferent to their plight and suffer greater anxiety, depression and school avoidance. Girls place greater value on social harmony than boys, and suffer greater anxiety and depression when their teachers respond with *passive* interventions (Simmons, 2002). In our increasingly litigious society, children must understand that bullying will not be tolerated and will be addressed *actively*. Not only do children deserve decisive action, but parents will, and should, demand it. Being safe is a fundamental human right all children deserve.

Who are the victims?

Children who are different in any way, such as physical appearance, personality or interests, are at greater risk of being bullied. Overly passive children with poor body language or inadequate social skills are also targeted (Grose, 2000). As Field (2007, p. 175) concludes: 'Most kids judge each other in the first four seconds.' Explicitly teaching children strong body language (see Chapter 7) and assertiveness (see Chapter 8) increases their confidence and helps to shield them from bullying. Other common victims of bullying are children who are shy or oversensitive, high or underachievers, overweight or members of a minority group, such as same-sex attracted and gender questioning (SSAGQ) children. Homophobia is one of the most common causes of bullying (Birkett et al., 2009). Sixty-one per cent of SSAGQ children report verbal abuse, 18 per cent report physical abuse and 26 per cent report other forms of homophobia (Hillier et al., 2010). Disturbingly, Hillier and colleagues (2010) discovered increasing levels of reported homophobic violence in schools, with 80 per cent of SSAGQ young people naming school as the most common location for bullying. More than half of the young people, who eventually identify as gay, know they are same-sex attracted at primary school. This equates to 6 per cent of the primary school population (Hillier et al., 2010). Primary schools must, therefore, consider the implications of not including same-sex issues in school policies on bullying.

A staggering 93 per cent of children have witnessed bullying (Eisen & Engler, 2007). This is a frightening statistic when we know that witnesses can be deeply scarred, and must certainly be counted as victims of bullying. Children who witness bullying are at higher risk of disliking school and wanting to stay home. They often experience higher levels of fear, anxiety, depression, hopelessness and inferiority than either bullies or victims (Beane, 2008; Rivers et al., 2009).

It is important to remember that bullies also need support. They frequently have inflated self-esteem, a need for power and control, lack strong friendships and have poor communication and conflict-resolution skills (Peters Mayer, 2008). Despite the fact that some may have a group of followers, they have poor social and emotional intelligence.

Strategies to address bullying

▶ Whole-school based programs to prevent bullying and promote prosocial behaviour are the most successful (Field, 2007). This must be underpinned by building school cultures where all stakeholders see bullying as unacceptable. Policies must be clear. Children must know what is unacceptable, what to do and who to go to. Trust grows from knowing that infringements have consequences and that teachers will act.

▶ Teach children to be ethical, caring and compassionate through taking responsibility for the safety and wellbeing of each other. Make it clear that witnesses of bullying must act by either reporting this to teachers or, when possible, asking the bully to stop. Children who witness bullying can be afraid to intervene fearing they might lose friends or become victims themselves. When school rules mandate that witnesses must confront or report bullying, this gives these children a sanctioned reason to act, releasing them from personal blame.

▶ Actively help children acquire friendship-making skills (see Chapter 8). Having even one supportive friend can protect victimised children from the negative effects of bullying (Troop-Gordon & Quenette, 2010).

▶ KidsMatter, our online national mental health initiative, provides excellent resources to promote children's mental health and wellbeing and protect them from bullying (see <http://www.kidsmatter.edu.au/primary/>).

▶ Children, from a young age, are discouraged from telling tales and many fear that confiding in someone may exacerbate the situation (Beane, 2008). Implement strategies for frightened children to report bullying without fear of being identified.

Developing a culture of encouraging students to not stand by during bullying is one of the most important steps to reducing the likelihood and harm from these incidents. Research shows that peer intervention to reduce bullying is very effective. When compared to an adult, if peers intervene, it is more likely the bullying will stop faster, there's less harm to the person being bullied and reconciliation between the students involved happens more quickly. Intervention by bystanders happens when schools set an ethos that says: 'This is the way we behave in our school, this is the expectation. If you stand and watch you are contributing to bullying.' Within a safe environment at the classroom level, specifically giving young people opportunities to practise ways to be a supportive bystander is important. They can learn socially credible ways to talk and act when bullying occurs.

PROFESSOR DONNA CROSS, CHILD HEALTH RESEARCH CENTRE, EDITH COWAN UNIVERSITY

▶ Ensure that parents are aware of the school's bullying policy and have confidence that the school will act. Well-informed parents are more supportive of efforts to address what can be extremely volatile and complicated situations.

John was always a happy child who naturally loved school. He was more academic than sporty, had an effervescent personality and most of his friends were girls. The teasing began in Year 2 because he had different interests to the other boys. He was resilient and tried to face it on his own until the pack mentality became worse. Continual name-calling, teasing, exclusion, kicking and punching were taking their toll. John was coming home distressed and sometimes refused to attend school. When he finally told us about the bullying, we contacted his teacher who was unaware of any of it. She tried to help but the bullying never really stopped. John became reluctant to confide in her due to threats of retribution by the boys and a fear of the teacher not believing him. On the last day of Year 2 we received the class list for the following year. My heart sank when I saw the names. I could not face another year of bullying. No, what I should be saying was, 'John cannot face another year like this.' With tears in my eyes and a choked-up voice, I rang the principal and poured my heart out. He listened intently and immediately reassured me that we could resolve this. He put strategies into place such as classes promoting prosocial behaviour and resilience, and he included the school psychologist and informed all staff. I felt the weight of despair start to lift because someone had listened, taken my concerns seriously and was prepared to help.

CAROL, **MOTHER OF JOHN, 11**

NEWSLETTER ITEM

Understanding cyberbullying

We must all recognise the warning signs that children are being cyberbullied. Does your child appear to be secretive, more upset, angry or sad after spending time online? Has your child suddenly started to avoid using the computer or checking emails? Talk to your child about cyberbullying and make sure the message is clear: all forms of bullying are unacceptable and must not be tolerated. Tell your child that a person being bullied must tell someone because this is the first and most important step to stopping it. Bullying in any form is unacceptable in our school. Working together, we can make school and home a safer place for our children. There are many excellent government websites providing information on cyberbullying.

Angry and aggressive children

Anger is a strong and frightening emotion for children. Angry and aggressive children are rarely happy or able to enjoy school and form healthy relationships. Seeing children explode, or meltdown in anger, makes for a very bad day at the office for teachers and other children in the class. Fifty-seven per cent of primary teachers have experienced aggression or threatening body language from students, 38 per cent have been verbally threatened with physical harm and 32 per cent have been pushed, shoved or have experienced physical violence (Galaxy Research, 2011).

Children's anger and aggression must be addressed as early as possible. Unless intervention strategies are put into place *before* Year 3, these children face bleak futures. They are at heightened risk of ongoing aggression, school dropout, delinquency and even adult incarceration (Whitted, 2011). Children with very high levels of aggression in early years show the largest decline in aggression when provided with intensive teacher support (Hughes & Kwok, 2006). This is another example of the enormous power teachers have to positively change short- and long-term outcomes for children.

There are a number of reasons why some children start school full of uncontrolled anger. Children, rejected by peers in early childhood, become increasingly aggressive in later childhood years (Hubbard, 2001). Anger and aggression often mask underlying issues such as depression, anxiety, family problems, bullying or even conflict with peers. Teachers can help enormously by discovering what is making children behave in these socially unhealthy ways. Angry and aggressive children often come from homes where there are few boundaries and consequences for poor behaviour or where parents have poor anger management. Children model what they see. Uninvolved parenting and harsh authoritarian parenting (see Chapter 3) both lead to children developing increased relational aggression (Kawabata et al., 2011). Children from these negative home environments are more aggressive because life is frustrating and difficult for them. Teachers face a difficult task in helping these children unlearn destructive expressions of anger and adopt socially acceptable and healthier ways of handling it. Children whose parents are warm but firm have higher levels of wellbeing and much lower levels of aggression. There is also strong evidence that repeated exposure to violent video games and violent television programs increases children's immediate and long-term aggression with the effects being greatest on children younger than 6, particularly boys (Wilson, 2008).

At school, children may become angry or aggressive when a goal is blocked or a need is frustrated. Daily classroom events such as conflict over possessions, pushing, hitting, teasing or exclusion from peer activities are hurtful and can provoke anger in children. By the age of 8, many children expect little emotional support from parents and peers should they feel angry as most are socialised to accept that expressing anger is inappropriate (Zeman & Shipman, 1996). Consequently, children learn to internalise anger or express it in nonverbal ways, such as mild aggressive behaviour. When children have no healthy outlet for anger, self-destructive behaviour frequently results (Brazelton & Sparrow, 2005). Integral to expressing anger appropriately is an understanding of anger itself (Zeman & Shipman, 1996) and having a repertoire of positive coping skills. In Dodge's social information processing model (Dodge, 1986), children's behaviour is affected first by their reading and interpretation of social cues, followed by their choice of response from their existing repertoire of possible responses. However, a child may inaccurately read an act as being intentionally hostile or aggressive, and then feel wronged and justified in reacting with anger and aggression (Dodge & Coie, 1987). Perception *is* reality. Aggressive children are more likely to make inaccurate interpretations of situations and lack skills required to react positively to negative situations. Teachers must help angry and aggressive children acknowledge that they have a tendency to read situations negatively. These children need practice interpreting emotions, body language and social situations more accurately (see Chapter 4). Cognitive Behaviour Therapy (CBT) steps similar to those mentioned for the anxious child can also be very effective in helping children deal with their anger (Attwood, 2004a).

There is a growing recognition that girls and boys express anger differently. Boys tend to display aggression physically, while girls frequently display relationally manipulative behaviours (Crick et al., 2007). Relational aggression involves harming others through spreading hurtful rumours or excluding them from activities. Teachers must be particularly vigilant in detecting girls' covert displays of anger and aggression, which are very destructive when channelled into bullying behaviour. Studies also show that, frequently, girls' expression of anger is ignored while boys' angry behaviour receives attention (Brody & Hall, 1993). Teachers should guard against overlooking girls' anger and strive to teach all children to handle and express anger in socially acceptable ways. Ignoring even mild displays of girls' anger is a lost opportunity to help them develop greater emotional literacy while initiating discussions about the underlying causes of their anger.

Although teachers are well-trained to address children's academic skill deficits, many feel ill-equipped to handle angry, disruptive and aggressive children. Some respond with punitive disciplinary measures, which only exacerbate children's negative behaviour (Whitted, 2011; see also Chapter 11). This is understandable, given how frustrating and emotionally taxing it is to deal with such challenging children, sometimes on a daily basis. However, the reality is that for the health and wellbeing of teachers and all children in the class, solution-oriented strategies need to be found, tried and sometimes re-tried. Always ensure that consequences are fair and consistent. Talk children through incidents, sending the message that even when behaviour is inappropriate, they are still valued.

Strategies to support angry and aggressive children

▶ Remind children that there is nothing wrong with feeling anger but it must be managed and expressed appropriately.

▶ Children who can express anger verbally are less likely to exhibit inappropriate behaviour (Whitted, 2011). Demystify anger by openly discussing this emotion and its consequences.

▶ Work hard to forge positive relationships with angry and aggressive children. This requires enormous teacher energy, but warm and supportive teaching can reduce negative behaviour (Cadima et al., 2010; Hughes & Kwok, 2006).

▶ Help children identify the triggers that make them feel angry, such as when they lose a game or someone calls them names. Teachers can then help children prepare for these situations by rehearsing coping strategies such as self-talk (see Chapter 5), counting to 10 or moving away.

▶ Prevent children from spiralling out of control so that they can avoid what Daniel Goleman calls 'emotional hijacking' (1996, p. 61). Teach them to recognise physiological signs of anger, such as sweating hands, heart racing and feeling hot or breathless. Recognising physical warning signs prompts children to implement coping and self-calming strategies to maintain control. Strategies include breathing slowly, counting to 10, moving away from the situation, thinking positive thoughts, allowing time to cool down and dropping 'angries' on the ground.

▶ Teach the difference between passive, aggressive and assertive behaviour (see Chapter 8).

▶ Introduce 'positive contract cards' to assist self-management. Children can tick these each day when they have achieved their aim of responding appropriately rather than aggressively.

▶ Encourage participation in extracurricular activities, which often improve children's behaviour (Guest & Schneider, 2003). Success in any endeavour promotes higher self-esteem and can help children turn that corner and want to behave more positively.

▶ When behaviour is extreme, or angry children are not responding to classroom strategies, consultation with welfare staff and parents is essential.

Special kids

Overwhelmingly, the trend is to integrate children with disabilities into mainstream primary schools. In any school, there may be several children who have a variety of disabilities: physical, cognitive, social or emotional. These special children have needs that can be challenging for already busy teachers. Supporting and nurturing these children so that they can gain important social and emotional skills requires a high level of teacher expertise, patience and professional knowledge.

It would be hoped that any teacher who has a child with a disability in their classroom is provided with support from the school administration. Schools should investigate whether children are eligible for funding to provide a teacher's aide and should give consideration to the make-up and size of the class. Getting to know these students' individual needs is imperative and assessments and reports from outside professionals, such as paediatricians, occupational therapists, speech pathologists, educational psychologists and educational optometrists, should be gathered from the family to help the teacher prepare programs.

As parents of a child with special needs, the following statement sums up what we need from educators: That you believe in our child, that you care and that you will act. If any part of this statement is lacking, then the child's opportunity to succeed, or feel worthy, will always be compromised.

In order for this to be a reality, educators must be supported with the following:

▶ *a school policy that clearly prioritises the pastoral and academic needs of children with specific needs*

> ▸ *access to professional development in the area of the child's diagnosis*
> ▸ *adequate time to meet with parents and share knowledge about the child*
> ▸ *appropriate classroom support from teacher aides and trained professionals.*

ROB AND KATHRYN, PARENTS

Attention deficit hyperactivity disorder (ADHD)

One of the fastest-growing groups of special kids is those diagnosed with attention deficit hyperactivity disorder (ADHD), which represents about 3 to 5 per cent of the school-age population (Stormont, 2008). Furthermore, approximately 1 in 160 children aged 6 to 12 have an autism spectrum disorder (ASD). Most primary schools would have at least one child with ASD, with more boys than girls presenting (Fombonne, 2005; Wray & Williams, 2007). Children with ADHD usually show inattention, hyperactivity and impulsiveness. Although most young children may occasionally exhibit these behaviours, ADHD children exhibit them to a greater degree for their age. With reference to criteria outlined in the *Diagnostic and Statistical Manual of Mental Disorders IV* (American Psychological Association, 2000), the following signs in the table below may be evident.

Signs of attention deficit hyperactivity disorder (ADHD)

Inattention	Hyperactivity	Impulsivity
Fails to attend to details and finish tasks	Fidgets – is 'on the go'	Blurts out answers
Has difficulty sustaining attention and effort	Leaves their seat in the classroom	Has difficulty waiting for their turn
Does not appear to listen	Rushes about or climbs	Has difficulty working in groups
Loses things, is forgetful and has difficulty organising tasks	Has difficulty playing quietly	Interrupts or intrudes on others
Is distracted by extraneous stimuli	Talks excessively	Rushes through set tasks

Some children with ADHD may have been prescribed medication and ideally parents should share this information with teachers. Teachers with these special kids in their class can then implement strategies that will also be beneficial for every child. These strategies include:

▶ checking seating arrangements so that children have minimal distractions

▶ maintaining a consistent, organised classroom structure

▶ preparing children for transitions from one lesson to another

▶ setting clear learning expectations

▶ using visual supports to assist learning

▶ minimising noise levels

▶ creating an escape-valve activity for when children are particularly 'hyper', such as an errand or a job that allows movement.

Autism spectrum disorders (including Asperger's syndrome)

Children with an autism spectrum disorder (ASD) can have a wide range of developmental issues. These include having: significant difficulty communicating in a socially appropriate manner; difficulty interpreting social cues; narrow interests; repetitive behaviour; and often a sensitivity to certain smells, tastes and textures. Within the autism spectrum disorder, mainstream schools are most likely to encounter children with Asperger's syndrome (AS). Having an Asperger's child in the class can be extremely challenging for teachers and other children. Strong collaboration between the school, parents and health professionals will benefit everyone, not least the child with Asperger's.

Teachers who are knowledgeable about AS, and who exhibit patience and understanding with the child, will surely create good outcomes. Teachers with a thorough and considered understanding of the student's specific quirks and needs will do better still. The challenge involves balancing the needs of the child with those of the rest of the class. Disruptions can be frequent and parents of other children are not always understanding, especially when their child may go home with a slightly distorted version of events. Educating children in the class is essential. Discussions around the value of individual differences are important at all ages. For younger AS children, pressures can be alleviated through strategies such as providing a quiet space in the classroom for times when the child may feel overwhelmed, structuring play ideas for lunch time and designating a special position where X stands in line (for example, X is always third in the line).

Remember, a school day requires an enormous amount of processing for any child. Children with AS have double the amount to process when you take into account the work behind understanding basic social cues. They also require teachers with knowledge, understanding and patience. In turn, these teachers deserve medals!

JODIE WASSNER, SCHOOL COUNSELLOR AND CHILD/ADOLESCENT PSYCHOLOGIST

Asperger's children need explicit teaching to assist their social and emotional development. Many require individual social skills lessons. While teachers must individualise their approach to children with Asperger's, well-planned programs to support these children benefit the whole class. Asperger's children are extremely sensitive to the approach and demeanour of the classroom teacher. Information about classroom routines and how the child functions best should be shared with specialist teachers to maintain consistency. Anxiety about changed routines or new activities can be decreased by using Social Stories™ where teachers, or aides, talk through new activities step-by-step. Recording steps in written form, accompanied by the child's illustrations, provides a document (security blanket) that children can refer back to when needed. Social Stories™ are a promising intervention, being relatively straightforward, efficient and useful for a wide range of behaviours (Reynhout & Carter, 2006). Social Stories™ are also increasingly used for mainstream classes, particularly with young children who may be anxious. Improved understanding of events, expectations and social information offers children reassurance and leads to more effective and appropriate behaviour.

Most Asperger's children respond well to visual cues, such as schedules, models of how finished tasks should look or graphic timetables (e.g. a playground supervision roster with teachers' photos), because their visual memory works more efficiently than their auditory memory. Too many verbal instructions or complicated explanations are lost on these children who take what is said literally. So be careful what you ask for and never be sarcastic. Children with Asperger's often do not understand displays of authority or anger, and may react with negative or stubborn behaviour. Provide a quiet space when these children become overwhelmed, being careful never to escalate power struggles. They rarely have positive outcomes. Assist Asperger's children to gain confidence, understanding of classroom social expectations and become more socially competent.

Here are some examples of strategies to achieve this:

▶ 'Catch' them being good, give immediate praise and ignore minor negative behaviours.
▶ Provide frequent physical breaks to move around (hand out or collect materials).
▶ Provide explicit and integrated opportunities to see, learn about and practise empathy towards others.
▶ Manage their return to the classroom after an absence by progressively increasing the number of hours they attend each day.

Both ADHD and Asperger's children require intensive time and energy. However, as they display growing social competence and acceptance from their peers, everyone benefits: these children, their classmates and teachers themselves.

Language disorders

Many primary school children are identified by parents or teachers with speech and/or language difficulties, affecting their ability to produce sounds, structure sentences and communicate with others. Unless addressed early, difficulties can continue into later school years affecting social interactions, academic results and bringing children unnecessary angst and embarrassment. In some cases, children may experience bullying as a result of their communication difficulties and so withdraw from peers. Undoubtedly, the resulting lack of confidence will prevent many children from developing into healthy, happy and gregarious young people.

Children with speech and/or language difficulties may present with the following:

▶ unclear speech that is difficult to understand
▶ an inability to find and use the right word; using non-specific words when talking ('The thing that goes there')
▶ taking a long time to think of the right words to say
▶ difficulty following verbal instructions and reliance on other cues (watching peers)
▶ difficulty understanding the social use of language (turn-taking in conversations).

Teachers discuss their students' language acquisition under the headings of receptive language, expressive language and articulation (physical). *Receptive language* is the ability to hear and comprehend what is being said. Some children, particularly boys, suffer from auditory processing problems (Rowe & Rowe, 2000) and can appear to lack attention and motivation. Early identification can break the cycle leading to acting out behaviours and help children gain confidence in social situations. Children must also be able to hear clearly, so a hearing test is imperative, especially for those children who suffer from constant colds. But even children with no physical problems may have difficulties in receiving and processing messages accurately.

Expressive language is the ability to express thoughts in well-structured words and sentences that make sense to listeners. Vocabulary and sentences should increase in complexity with the child's age. Good *articulation* involves the ability to use and place the tongue appropriately to produce a proper sound. All young children, when they are just learning to speak, mispronounce words; but as they grow older, their articulation skills develop and their pronunciation usually becomes clearer. Many teachers use the Cued Articulation Method (Passy, 2010), or parts thereof, which provides visual cues of each sound. Colourful Semantics (Bryan, 2008) is another program which many teachers find useful when assisting children with language difficulties. Teachers who are concerned that a child is not showing any improvement should approach parents to discuss a possible referral to a speech pathologist who will evaluate the child's oral and/or written language skills and suggest support strategies.

High achieving and gifted kids

High achievers and gifted children can feel frustrated at school unless challenged and supported to achieve a sense of success (Baum & Owen, 2004). Gifted children can also suffer from 'asynchrony' as their intellectual skills develop more rapidly than physical and/or emotional ones, leaving them socially and emotionally unbalanced. Early identification and support of gifted children can make school immensely more enjoyable for them and boost their social and emotional development (Eisen & Engler, 2007).

At even greater risk of diminished social and emotional development are the gifted but learning-disabled children who, as a unique group of students, are under-identified. These children present as: extremely clever students who are not achieving their expected standards; students who show aspects of giftedness in specific areas of their learning; and those who mask their gifts and appear average (Krochak & Ryan, 2007). Children with ability/disability can display frustration, anger, depression, carelessness and off-task behaviour and be disruptive in class. Difficult to identify, they can be prevented from reaching their full potential academically, socially and emotionally. Teachers should not hesitate to seek support from school welfare staff that may organise a professional assessment.

The 'a little left of centre' kids

A group of 'special kids' who sometimes slip under the radar are those who are cooperative and present no behavior problems, but are concealing huge personal problems. These children often don't know how to ask for help. Their social and emotional development will be held back unless sharp-eyed teachers identify their unhappiness and find them appropriate support.

It's the end of the first term at high [secondary] school for the new Year 7s and most have found their niche in the friendship arena. The bell rings and the room quickly empties as students flood into the corridor for recess. As usual, Andrew lags behind. Once in the corridor, he moves to his usual spot, slumps cross-legged onto the floor and takes a novel from his bag. Focusing intently on the pages, he 'disappears' into another world. The same pattern is repeated every recess and every lunchtime. Classmates have tried to strike up conversations with Andrew, but his cool and aloof manner have quickly made him a no-go zone. His English teacher notices the dark and disturbing drawings covering his school diary. After several meetings with the student counsellor, we discover that Andrew's father moved out over the last school holidays and his mother was diagnosed with bipolar disorder. Andrew isn't antisocial or disinterested in school; in his own way he is mourning the loss of his father and the loss of his mother's health. He will need special care, patience and understanding from his teachers as he adjusts to a new and difficult home situation.

MICHELLE, YEAR 7 TEACHER

Some children do enjoy quiet time alone, but many are escaping from difficult situations. If children are seen sitting alone regularly, it is important for teachers to check why they are withdrawing from the social milieu. Is it due to unhappiness relating to difficult circumstances, being ostracised by peers or a lack of social skills preventing them from confidently joining groups? Other children are just a little different from the 'average' child in the class. They don't quite fit. These can be happy children who have often grown up predominantly with adults or older siblings. They can have a more sophisticated outlook or dryer sense of humour that can put them a little out of kilter with peers. Teachers can support these children by helping them to see how their words and actions can be misunderstood. These children become less noticeable as they progress through primary school and other children catch up and become more mature.

eleven

Head and heart matters

Depression

It is well recognised that there are rising levels of depression in children and adolescents (Seligman, 2008), large increases in the number of children being prescribed anti-depressants (Parkinson & Kazzi, 2011) and alarming increases in suicidal behaviour in children as young as 10 to 14 (Eckert et al., 2003). Very recent research confirms that children as young as 3 can suffer from depression (Luby, 2010).

Teaching children social skills is one of the most powerful strategies teachers have to protect them from depression (see Chapters 7 to 9). Children who see themselves as being socially competent possess a strong protective barrier against depression, even if they are at an increased risk due to other life events (Andrews et al., 2001). Children who are shy and socially withdrawn also suffer from depression as well as loneliness and anxiety (Rubin et al., 2009).

Children are not as articulate as adults and sometimes are confused and frightened by feelings they are powerless to control or understand. Because children spend so much time each day at school, teachers are ideally placed to identify those exhibiting early symptoms of that 'something not quite right' behaviour, which could signal depression.

SIGNS OF DEPRESSION

▶ A prevailing sadness, moodiness, unexplained crying, becoming fearful, anxious and tense, feelings of guilt and complaining about boredom

- Uncooperative behaviour in class, restlessness and irritability, easily upset or annoyed, sudden outbursts of anger
- Expressing negative thoughts, 'catastrophic thinking', feelings of hopelessness and worthlessness
- Impaired memory and lack of motivation, energy and ability to concentrate
- Withdrawing from social contact and spending more time alone
- Loss of interest in previously-enjoyed activities or sometimes excessive involvement in a particular activity (e.g. playing computer games)
- Missing days at school and declining results
- Physical deterioration (e.g. tiredness, aches and pains, minor illnesses, significant weight gain or loss)
- Unnecessary risk-taking (more so with older children)
- Self-harming or talking, writing about and drawing images of death and suicide

Note: Children with 5 or more of these signs for at least 2 weeks – with no sign of the 'flatness' lifting – may be suffering from depression and professional help must be provided.

Clearly, the most concerning signs are self-harming and talking about suicide; however, any significant or unexplained change in a child's usual behaviour could also be a warning sign. Teachers should immediately speak to parents and seek advice from school counsellors, welfare staff and the principal. Early identification and support for children exhibiting 'out of character' symptoms can prevent them from developing clinical depression and from being more vulnerable to episodes of depression as adolescents and adults (Luby, 2010). It is important to remember that sometimes depression in young children can go undetected by parents and teachers because the symptoms are often not disruptive. Beware the compliant child who may little by little withdraw from friends and appear detached from activities. The teacher who can put the pieces of the puzzle together can activate support and rescue a child from slipping into depression.

Causes of depression

Causes of depression in children are complicated. Rather than a single factor being the catalyst, multiple factors or cumulative adverse life events combine to put children at risk (Burns et al., 2002). Some possible causes are: a lack of resilience; poor social skills resulting in difficulty making friends and peer connections; negativity and learned helplessness; parents fighting, separating or divorcing, particularly when this is acrimonious (Seligman, 2007); death of a loved one and other significant losses; physical, verbal or emotional abuse, including bullying. Children who have a depressed parent are four times more likely to develop depression (Burns et al., 2002), with maternal mental illness being more detrimental than paternal illness (Meadows et al., 2007). Knowing that children have one or more of these issues should alert teachers to be more watchful of them. Numerous studies show the relationship between bullying and depression and both victims and bullies are affected (Klomek et al., 2007). Schools can protect children from anxiety and depression by implementing a zero-tolerance bullying policy.

Occasionally children become caregivers for parents who, for a variety of reasons, are unable to fulfil the normal parental role. Some of these situations include temporary or chronic illness, disabled parents or parents with a mental illness or addiction. In some situations, older children may also be caring for younger siblings. Whether temporary or permanent, these situations place enormous responsibility on young shoulders. 'Parentification' or 'adultification' of children causes high levels of stress, anxiety and sometimes depression (East, 2010). If teachers believe that a child may be anxious or depressed due to excessive home responsibilities, this should be discussed with school welfare staff and the principal so that children and families can be supported.

Video game use has introduced a new threat to children's mental health. In the United States, approximately 8.5 per cent of gamers are classified as 'pathological' and experience poorer grades at school, increased hostility, ADHD and depression. Gamers are pathological when playing interferes with everyday life. In Australia, 11.9 per cent of gamers fall into this category (Gentile et al., 2011). Initially, researchers assumed that children retreat into games to handle feeling anxious or depressed. This is now seen as an oversimplification. Some children do use games as a coping mechanism, which increases their levels of depression. Many more, however, *become* pathological gamers and then develop higher levels of anxiety, social phobia and depression. When gamers overcome their addiction, levels of anxiety, social phobia and depression decrease. Although most of the gaming happens at home, teachers will see the fallout at school, particularly in children's fatigue, anger, lack of attention or possible withdrawal. Teachers who form the belief that a child is spending too much time online, or is becoming addicted to gaming, must discuss this with parents so that they understand the negative impact this can have on their child.

Strategies to prevent children from developing depression

▶ Prevention is always better than cure. Teaching children optimistic thinking skills can halve the rate of depression that occurs during puberty and in later life (O'Rourke & Cooper, 2010). Teachers can protect children who have uncontrolled negativity and catastrophic thinking (Clark & Beck, 2010) by teaching cognitive skills (Burns et al., 2002) that develop optimistic and realistic thinking (see Chapter 5).

▶ Teaching problem solving reduces children's depression (Pincus & Friedman, 2004; see also Chapter 9).

▶ Maintain open communication with parents. By knowing about significant disruptions to a child's life, teachers can offer additional support and patience when children need it. A good partnership between school and home is essential when a child is suffering from anxiety or depression. Progress will go up and down and teachers need to be sensitive and attuned to how a child is 'travelling' so that they can respond and support appropriately.

▶ Encourage children to participate in extracurricular activities as these engage them with school (Spence et al., 2005) and generally provide opportunities for important social interaction, which is a buffer against depression.

▶ KidsMatter is an excellent online framework for school-based programs that can help prevent depression by promoting emotional wellbeing and resilience. Many resources focus on teaching problem solving, leadership, optimism, positive thinking and communication. These programs often require teachers to gain professional development.

Body image and eating disorders

An unhealthy preoccupation with body image is no longer just the domain of adolescents but is a growing concern for primary school children and can develop into eating disorders such as anorexia nervosa and bulimia nervosa.

Eating disorders are more dangerous in children than in adolescents and adults as they can permanently stunt growth and development (Rosen, 2010). They are serious and can be life-threatening.

From 1999 to 2006, hospitalisations for eating disorders increased most sharply: 119 per cent for children younger than 12 (Rosen, 2010). Forty-one per cent of children are specifically worried about the way they look, with 35 per cent concerned about being overweight (44 per cent of girls and 27 per cent of boys) and 16 per cent concerned about being too skinny (Tucci et al., 2007).

> *Kindergarten children talk about dieting and one of the worst things they can call someone is fat. They hear about dieting from other children, the media and parents who are well-meaning, but preschoolers can be too young to understand positive messages. Some have extreme responses such as ceasing to eat or becoming scared of certain foods. One child at kindergarten was told that something in her lunchbox could give her a heart attack and she would only eat fruit and vegetables after that.*
>
> **DR NAOMI CRAFTI, PSYCHOLOGIST**

Genetic predisposition and personality may play a part in some children developing an eating disorder, particularly those who are anxious, high achievers or perfectionists. Boys and girls with low self-esteem are also more vulnerable to developing eating disorders. But why are levels of eating disorders rising in children? Many see the media as playing a major part. The average child in the United Kingdom, the United States and Australia sees between 20 000 and 40 000 television advertisements per year. Bombarded with images about how they should look, children form narrow and dangerous images of what constitutes beauty. Struggling to fit these views, children suffer from anxiety, stress and lower self-acceptance (Williams, 2006). Female thinness, overvalued and equated with beauty, success and happiness, has led to widespread body dissatisfaction among adolescent girls (Paquette & Raine, 2004) and even girls as young as 6 (Davison et al., 2003). Girls as young as 5 fear gaining weight and 67 per cent of anorexic children who are hospitalised have misperceptions of their body shape (Madden et al., 2009). Children whose parents transmit messages about the importance of thinness are more likely to develop concerns with their own weight and shape (Davison & Lipps Birch,

2001). Interestingly, well-intentioned parental messages ('Should you eat that extra piece?') are more potent predictors of body dissatisfaction in adolescents than parental teasing (Helfert & Warschburger, 2011). These subtle messages can subliminally play on children's minds.

The number of children we are seeing with eating disorders is increasing each year. Children as young as 5 are being diagnosed with eating disorders. Many are presenting for treatment so sick they have to be hospitalised. It is concerning that children are being referred so late when they are already suffering from severe complications associated with their starvation, with some even at risk of dying. There are a number of reasons why children are presenting with eating disorders younger than ever before. They are being exposed to images of thinness at a much, much younger age and to sexualised images at an age when they are psychologically unable to understand those images.

Early identification is essential. Teachers can help both to increase children's resilience to eating disorders and to identify children at risk. They can help to prevent eating disorders by delivering balanced and positive messages around body image, with a focus on healthy eating and activity rather than size and shape, and helping children challenge negative body image messages from the media. In terms of identifying children at risk for eating disorders, teachers must be aware that these illnesses can affect both boys and girls at a young age. Children with eating concerns will often start to isolate themselves from their peers, particularly around eating, become more irritable and withdrawn and in some cases start to focus excessively on food, exercise and health.

DR SLOANE MADDEN, HEAD OF DEPARTMENT OF EATING DISORDERS, WESTMEAD CHILDREN'S HOSPITAL

Eating disorders are difficult to detect as sufferers often carefully hide their behaviour and appearance. Significant weight loss can remain hidden for some time even from the most caring and observant parents and teachers. Teachers can protect children by being vigilant at lunchtimes and ensuring that uneaten food is returned home in the lunchbox, perhaps with a note asking parents to speak to the child about why the food isn't being eaten. Significant weight loss and signs of vomiting after eating are concerning, and teachers must broach concerns with parents who may be unaware of what is happening. Denial is not uncommon when parents are understandably frightened. Importantly, teachers are not doctors and should always tread purposefully, but gently; for example, 'Is Alex unwell and vomiting due to a food allergy? Could there be other reasons Alex isn't eating?' Teachers and parents should remain in communication to offer children the best support.

SIGNS OF EATING DISORDERS

▶ Significant weight loss in a relatively short time
▶ Wearing baggy clothes to hide weight loss
▶ Obsession with weight and calories
▶ Exercising excessively
▶ Frequent trips to the bathroom after eating
▶ Anxiety about food or avoiding situations where food is being eaten
▶ Eating very slowly or pretending to have already eaten
▶ Pale appearance, dizziness, headaches, moodiness, tiredness, inability to concentrate
▶ Light bruising under the eyes

Obesity and overweight children

While many children starve themselves to resemble waif-like idols, others are lured by the many fast food ads. Since the 1970s, obesity has more than doubled for children aged 2 to 5, and tripled for children aged 6 to 11 in the United States (Barros et al., 2009). In Australia, 1 in every 4 children is overweight, with 5 to 8 per cent identified as obese (Gill et al., 2009; Olds et al., 2010). Although the prevalence of overweight and obesity seems to have stabilised, an unacceptable number of children are affected and teachers must be aware of the alarming consequences for these children. Overweight children are generally more socially isolated and have fewer friends, which negatively affects emotional development (Strauss & Pollack, 2003). This is particularly serious, given that relationships and peer acceptance increase in importance each year and underpin children's ability to form a healthy identity. A study of 5-year-old girls revealed that those with higher weight status had lower body-esteem and negative *perceptions* of their academic and athletic ability (Davison & Lipps Birch, 2001). Teachers need to be on their guard to protect overweight children from overt and covert teasing or exclusion. To redress how these children are often negatively perceived by their peers (as well as themselves) teachers can identify their special strengths and talents and find ways to highlight these within the classroom. Clearly, teachers must be sensitive to the needs of overweight children if they are to nurture their social and emotional wellbeing.

> *Obesity results in immediate and serious long-term health consequences in children and adolescents. These range from orthopaedic complications, sleep apnoea, cardiovascular disease risk factors, type 2 diabetes and psychosocial problems, including low self-esteem and depression. Many of these ill-health consequences also apply to children and adolescents who are overweight. Early intervention is important. Teachers can help by encouraging and supporting healthy eating and active lifestyles among children through classroom and school activities. A healthy school canteen menu shows children appropriate food choices and indicates the importance their school places on maintaining a healthy weight.*
>
> **ASSOCIATE PROFESSOR TIMOTHY GILL, INSTITUTE OF OBESITY, NUTRITION AND EXERCISE AND EATING DISORDERS, UNIVERSITY OF SYDNEY**

Appearance is a hot topic of conversation even among primary children. 'Unacceptable' appearance can lead to exclusion from social networks and activities, particularly for overweight individuals (Strauss & Pollack, 2003). Evidence suggests that boys are more likely than girls to initiate weight-based teasing and harassment of other children (Stein, 1999). An American research project used puppet programs with junior primary children to promote an acceptance of diverse body shapes. Tackling anti–fat attitudes *early* can prevent these attitudes becoming firmly entrenched in young minds. This is an important preventative measure as these negative attitudes contribute to teasing and a preoccupation with weight and shape (Irving, 2000).

> *Childhood obesity is an issue demanding urgent attention. The health problems, stigmatisation and costs of obesity are significant, both now and into our children's future. It's sad, but true, that obese children are subjected to bias and discrimination and this occurs not just by rejection from other children in the playground, but often in the classroom too. Research shows that teachers may reflect society's negative attitudes and unintentionally treat overweight children differently. Children may also experience*

humiliation and derogatory comments from other professionals including doctors, nurses and dietitians. Even parents have been shown to give less financial support to their obese children's tertiary education. Ultimately, the social, economic and psychological consequences can be significant, negatively affecting school performance, tertiary acceptance, psychosocial functioning and virtually all aspects of life. A very heavy burden indeed.

ASSOCIATE PROFESSOR JOHN DIXON, HEAD OF OBESITY RESEARCH UNIT, MONASH UNIVERSITY

Research mentioned by Professor Dixon should prompt every teacher to undertake careful soul searching. Teachers can be influenced by pervasive and unrelenting societal stigmatisation of overweight people with many believing that overweight children are more untidy and less likely to succeed than other children (Puhl & Latner, 2007). Subconscious discrimination by teachers and parents may cause children lasting emotional damage and make social situations uncomfortable and feared. Every primary school would have some overweight or obese children and teachers must ensure that messages are balanced, sensitively delivered and non-judgemental. All children should be encouraged to participate in physical activity and to eat healthy food with the focus being on health and fitness rather than body shape and weight.

Strategies to promote healthy body image and weight

- Classroom discussions and programs can promote healthy eating habits. Avoid the word 'fat'.
- Promote the idea of healthy bodies rather than focusing on shape. Talk about fitness, not weight and appearance.
- Students in the middle and upper levels are entering their prepubescent years. Use this opportunity to discuss physical development. Stress that everyone is unique and there is no perfect size or shape.
- Encourage participation in sport and active play to increase fitness and prevent rising levels of overweight and obese children.

Prickly kids

Prickly kids are the 'stuff of nightmares' for teachers and are uncannily healthy. They are simply never sick! They are the primary cause for teacher burnout and psychological stress (Maag, 2008). Even one extremely difficult child can create chaos in the class. Oppositional children are tiring and constantly 'in your face'. Not surprisingly, many children who simply will not cooperate with teachers have poor social and emotional skills. Defiant, hyperactive and aggressive children typically have poor emotional regulation (Rydell et al., 2003). These children desperately need help if they are to succeed both at school and in the wider society.

Children may be prickly for many reasons. Those who come from homes where parents have few established boundaries are often captives of their own inability to respect social norms, including classroom expectations. They are also often reluctant to accept directives from teachers. Unrealistically high parental expectations, family problems or even being bullied can also make children so unhappy that they simply lash out in anger and become oppositional. When children are rejected by their peer group they can feel powerless to respond to this devastating situation, and many react by redirecting their anger and aggression onto other children or even teachers (Nesdale & Duffy, 2011). Some children exhibit disruptive behaviour because of an inability or perceived inability to succeed at school. Those who find work difficult may disguise this in the form of not caring about work at all. At the other end of the spectrum, children who are bored or under-challenged can become frustrated and oppositional. Teachers who can unearth the reasons behind prickliness gain invaluable insights into how to support these unhappy children.

More than half a century ago, behaviourist B. F. Skinner (1953) used the term 'countercontrol' to describe the deliberate actions of those being controlled to turn the tables and control their controllers. All teachers, at some point, recognise that a student is trying to upset them and goad them into a strong reaction through behaviour that includes subtle and persistent retorts and actions. Occurring across all types of schools, approximately 10 per cent of children engage in countercontrolling behaviour (Carey & Bourbon, 2004). Students countercontrol more frequently when teachers *tell* them to do something instead of *asking* them. Rather than saying 'Line up at the door and no talking', a more invitational approach such as 'Let's see how quickly and quietly we can all line up' will appear to be less controlling. Carey and Bourbon also discovered (2004, p. 5) that countercontrollers enjoy seeing teachers 'get mad', 'go off task' or 'yell and scream'. Sound familiar? In our experience, although contercontrollers can be found at all levels, they surface more during the later primary years when rules are harder to enforce due to children's desire to push the boundaries and impress peers rather than adults. Children who countercontrol are rarely happy. They frequently have inadequate social and emotional skills and countercontrol due to feeling disempowered or disengaged with school, peers or, sadly, even those at home. By consciously using *requests* rather than 'just do it because I say so' directives, teachers can reduce countercontrolling (and teacher stress) and increase cooperative behaviour. More than 80 years ago, psychotherapist Alfred Adler recognised that every child (and adult) has a fundamental need to belong if they are to be happy, have good mental health and exhibit prosocial behaviour (Dreikurs Ferguson, 2010). Making children feel that they truly belong should, therefore, underpin all support strategies and communication with prickly kids.

Although the negative behaviour of particular children may be irritating and frustrating, labelling them as bad or troublemakers will not improve the situation or make teaching easier. Labels stick. It is human nature for teachers and other children to begin treating children as the labels describe and, perhaps unconsciously, these children oblige by becoming what is expected of them. A more ethical and productive approach is for teachers to introduce strategies to assist troubled children. In addition to the teaching of essential social and emotional skills, the key to preventing children's unacceptable behaviour is quality teaching that is challenging and engaging. Boys are more disengaged with school and exhibit more behaviour problems than girls, often due to issues related to literacy (Rowe & Rowe, 2000). It is also important that teachers remember that boys typically have a higher prevalence of auditory processing issues than girls, which can lead to what appears to be bad behaviour (Rowe & Rowe, 2000; see also Chapter 7). Teachers must understand and cater for the preferred learning styles of boys. Boys generally need regular and positive reinforcement to promote achievement and improved behaviour. They enjoy competition and challenge, short tasks, frequent changes in activities and teacher-directed work rather than group work. Teachers can sometimes offer students choice in *how* they work and the activities undertaken, so that both boys and girls are engaged and less likely to be oppositional.

Teachers can more successfully handle difficult students by first examining their own response to very draining and upsetting behaviour. It is very easy for teachers to overreact emotionally, which only inflames the situation. Teachers can use rational–emotive therapy techniques to gain mastery over their own emotions and behaviours in the face of upsetting behaviour from children and learn to respond in more effective ways (Maag, 2008). This involves first identifying irrational beliefs ('If I can't control this child I am a failure') and learning to stop the tendency to catastrophise ('This child's behaviour is disastrous'). By controlling irrational thoughts, teachers stay composed, remain in control and refuse to engage in power struggles. Great teachers acknowledge what 'pushes their buttons' and work hard to navigate difficult situations with increasing skill. Emotions cannot be divorced from teaching. Teachers also need strategies to handle stress and relax after particularly demanding days. While they can often read children's emotions and notice signs of distress, many do not notice signs that they themselves may need support from colleagues and school leaders. Looking after teachers' social and emotional health is looking after children's social and emotional health.

Strategies to charm and tame prickly kids

▶ Teach children to use positive self-talk that will help them to think and behave more rationally (Banks & Zionts, 2009; see also Chapter 5). Children can be oppositional due to an inability to handle difficult emotions. Support them to identify and manage feelings, handle stress and solve problems (see Chapters 4, 5 and 9).

▶ Give children more choice in class to increase their feelings of ownership and autonomy, which in turn increases their motivation, enjoyment and even willingness to stay on task and overcome challenges (Nickolite & Doll, 2008; Patall et al., 2010). The opportunity to choose can make children feel their voice is heard, which increases their sense of ownership for rules and consequences and the likelihood they will work more cooperatively (Brooks & Goldstein, 2008).

▶ Discover the skills and interests the oppositional child has. Everyone, even the most difficult child, enjoys feeling special and knowing that the teacher is interested in them. Sometimes this can help an uncooperative child begin to want to turn that corner and work *with* rather than against teachers.

▶ The program TRIBES (Gibbs, 2006) provides a whole-school vision for building a cooperative community that can engage all children, but particularly oppositional children, through developing prosocial skills.

If negative behaviour remains unchanged despite intensive intervention and strategies, children should be referred for a behaviour assessment. Educational psychologists have a range of behaviour assessments that can be used to identify specific behaviour difficulties. Continuing to struggle without some support from school administration and outside agencies is not healthy or productive for teachers or children.

Prickly parents

Parental expectations of school have changed dramatically over the past 10 to 20 years. Parents today expect so much more of teachers and believe that schools should provide many things including: a wide curriculum; improved academic outcomes; accountability in regard to safety; sound social and emotional programs; and transparent assessment and reporting. While most parents remain wonderfully supportive, prickly parents can be very disturbing for teachers and dominate their attention and time. The worry this brings can affect teachers' emotional health and ability to teach effectively. Alarmingly, 50 per cent of teachers have experienced verbal abuse from parents (Galaxy Research, 2011). Parents who criticise and attack schools and teachers hinder their children's academic, social and emotional development. It is difficult for impressionable children to respect teachers when they hear them being condemned at home. This can undermine children's confidence in teachers and lead to uncooperative behaviour and even disengagement with school. Children are happier and more successful at school when parents and teachers work in partnership and avoid the cycle of blaming each other (O'Sullivan & Russell, 2006).

If teachers and parents can combine their efforts, they will be able to nurture children's wellbeing more successfully. To achieve this, teachers must strive to build a respectful and trusting relationship with the parents of their students. However, when communication breaks down, teachers dealing with prickly parents should always proceed with caution: prior to meetings prepare thoroughly and gather insights and information from other teachers. Are these parents always difficult? Have other teachers successfully established a positive rapport with them? Sometimes prickliness has nothing to do with school or teachers. Are serious home issues causing great distress and anxiety in the family? Is the child in question so difficult that the parent feels overwhelmed and is lashing out in frustration?

Teachers also need some insight into their own behaviour and communication. Has a respectful classroom environment been established? Are all children seen as individuals and valued for their abilities and strengths? Have parents been kept in the loop about issues concerning their children? Have promised actions been followed through? Teachers can often prevent relationships breaking down by proactively addressing situations before they escalate and by looking at issues through the eyes of parents. Even the most difficult of parents usually want the best outcomes for their children, as do teachers.

Strategies to tame prickly parents

▶ Smile and always begin conversations with a focus on children's strengths and achievements. Patience, patience, patience. Listen, listen, listen.

▶ Recognise parents as valuable partners and build relationships as early in the year as possible. This will provide a solid foundation to fall back on if prickly issues arise.

▶ Reassure parents that you are working in their child's best interests. To build parental trust, always explain the rationale behind particular interventions being implemented for their child. Ask parents for the strategies they use to deal with their child's organisation and behaviour to provide consistency between home and school: 'What do you do to encourage Chris to listen to instructions?' or 'When Tony gets angry at home, how do you calm him?'

▶ Don't limit communication to formal parent–teacher nights. Regularly communicating good news to parents builds goodwill and trust, which are invaluable if difficulties arise with a child's future behaviour or academic progress. Communication can be in the form of a note in a child's diary, an email or phone call and may also boost a child's self-esteem and result in more cooperative behaviour.

▶ Use your charm. You'll always catch more flies with honey than with vinegar! But, if all else fails, don't go home and face sleepless nights. Prickly parents are a school issue. Rather than face them alone, individual teachers should approach leadership for support.

gress res...
tion practice
ics foundation se...
personal we...
pathy individual progress
being values communication pr

Personal reflections

Never before has the work of primary teachers been so accountable, complex and demanding and under such public scrutiny.

The reality is that the world of childhood has become infinitely more complex and adultified. Take a look at what they are showing on music videos or browse through the websites and magazines targeted at young people. The influence of media and technology has permeated every aspect of our children's home and school lives. This means that, beyond classroom teaching, teachers now have the additional responsibility to address the impact of media and technology on children's self-esteem, identity formation and overall wellbeing.

Raising all children's academic outcomes can only be attained when teachers understand the pivotal role social and emotional development plays in children's academic success and have the skills and confidence to promote it.

It is precisely the recognition that children's social and emotional development must be addressed in schools that has prompted both state and federal governments to launch initiatives such as KidsMatter and other social and emotional learning (SEL) programs for primary teachers.

Because the world of teaching is changing at such a rapid pace, many teachers feel ill-equipped to face the increasing number of social and emotional problems exhibited by their students. This is leading to occupational stress, job dissatisfaction and attrition. Teachers themselves have identified a need for more intensive and ongoing professional development (Graham et al., 2011).

Schools must make professional development a priority, incorporating it into their strategic planning and school improvement process. Whole-school systematic approaches to planning and implementing social and emotional programs are more successful than an ad hoc delivery of programs.

Ongoing professional development is crucial when many pre-service teacher training courses do not adequately prepare teachers to deal with the complexities encountered in today's classrooms (Graham et al., 2011). Indeed, teacher training needs to focus on providing our future teachers with greater knowledge of children's social and emotional development, so they are prepared for real-life teaching as they step out of the university gates.

Social and emotional learning programs are most effective when parents are involved and support the work of teachers. Schools should actively engage and educate parents so they too have the strategies to help support their children's social and emotional development at home.

It is evident that the primary years are a crucial time when teachers have the greatest power to influence children's social and emotional development positively and, where necessary, to identify developmental deficits and offer early intervention strategies. This is when children are still malleable, thus offering teachers the greatest opportunity to guide and nurture their wellbeing.

Children's resilience, self-esteem and identity are not fixed. Children can learn the skills to become more socially and emotionally healthy and gain the inner strength required to meet the demands of the 21st century.

What we are seeing is a paradigm shift in the way we view education. Education is no longer just about literacy and numeracy. As teachers, our job is not only to impart knowledge from textbooks. Our power lies in the way we nurture little people and transform them into well-rounded human beings. Our power is reflected in the eyes of those we have taught who grow up into the thoughtful and self-assured adults we helped shape. Our power is also our responsibility.

Ros and Erin

References

Ablow, J. C., Measelle, J. R., Cowan, P. A., & Cowan. C. P. (2009). Linking marital conflict and children's adjustment: The role of young children's perceptions. *Family Psychology, 23*(4), 485–499.

Adams, H. (1999) [1907]. *The Education of Henry Adams.* New York: Oxford University Press.

American Psychiatric Association. (2000). *Diagnostic and statistical manual of mental disorders* (4th ed., DSM–IV). Washington, DC: Author.

Andrews, G., Szabo, M., & Burns, J. (2001). *Avertable risk factors for depression in young people. Is there enough evidence to warrant prevention programs?* Evaluation report. Melbourne and Sydney: beyondblue. Retrieved from http://www.beyondblue.org.au

Anfara, V. A. (2008). What the research says: Varieties of parent involvement in schooling. *Middle School Journal, 39*(3), 58–64.

Argyle, M. (2001). *The psychology of happiness.* New York: Routledge.

Arnon, S., Shamai, S., & Ilatov, Z. (2008). Socialization agents and activities of young adolescents. *Adolescence, 43*(170), 373–397.

Attwood, T. (2004a). *Exploring feelings: Cognitive behaviour therapy to manage anger.* Arlington, TX: Future Horizons.

Attwood, T. (2004b). *Exploring feelings: Cognitive behaviour therapy to manage anxiety.* Arlington, TX: Future Horizons.

Banks, T., & Zionts, P. (2009). Teaching a cognitive behavioural strategy to manage emotions. *Intervention in School and Clinic, 44*(5), 307–313.

Barrett, P. M., Lowry-Webster, H., & Turner, C. (2000). *FRIENDS program for children: Group leaders manual.* Brisbane: Academic Press.

Barros, R. M., Silver, E. J., & Stein, R. (2009). School recess and group classroom behavior. *Pediatrics, 123*(2), 431–436.

Baum, S. M., & Owen, S. V. (2004). *To be gifted and learning disabled: Strategies for helping bright students with learning and attention difficulties.* Mansfield, CT: Creative Learning.

Baumrind, D. (1966). Effects of authoritative parental control on child behavior. *Child Development, 37*(4), 887–907.

Beane, A. L. (2008). *Protect your child from bullying.* San Francisco: Jossey-Bass.

Bhagwan, R. (2009). Creating sacred experiences for children as pathways to healing, growth and transformation. *International Journal of Children's Spirituality, 14*(3), 225–234.

Birkett, M., Espelage, D. L., & Koenig, B. W. (2009). LGB and questioning students in schools: The moderating effects of homophobic bullying and school climate on negative outcomes. *Youth and Adolescence, 38*(7), 989–1000.

Blatt, M., & Kohlberg, L. (1975). The effects of classroom moral discussion upon children's level of moral judgement. *Moral Education, 4*(2), 129–161.

Bollmer, J. M., Milich, R., Harris, M. J., & Maras, M. A. (2005). A friend in need: The role of friendship quality as protective factor in peer victimisation and bullying. *Interpersonal Violence, 20*(6), 701–712.

Borg, J. (2008). *Body language: 7 easy lessons to master the silent language.* New York: Prentice Hall.

Brazelton, T, B., & Sparrow, J. D. (2005). *Mastering anger and aggression: The Brazelton way.* Cambridge, MA: Da Capo Press.

Brent, S. B., Speece, M. W., Lin, C., Dong, Q., & Yang, C. (1996). The development of the concept of death among Chinese and U.S. children 3–17 years of age: From binary to 'fuzzy' concepts? *Omega, 33*(1), 67–83.

Brody, J. E. (2010, November 29). Head out for a daily dose of green space. *The New York Times.* Retrieved from http://www.nytimes.com/2010/11/30/health/30brody.html

Brody, L. R., & Hall, J. A. (1993). Gender and emotion. In M. Lewis & J. Haviland (Eds.), *Handbook of Emotions* (pp. 447– 460). New York: Guilford Press.

Brooks, R., & Goldstein, S. (2008). The mindset of teachers capable of fostering resilience in students. *Canadian Journal of School Psychology, 23*(1), 114–126.

Brown, M. (2009). *Foundation blocks: Personal, social and emotional development.* Carlton South, VIC: Curriculum Corporation (Education Services Australia).

Bryan, A. (2008) Colourful semantics: Thematic role therapy. In S. Chait, J. Law, & J. Marshall (Eds.), *Language disorders in children and adults: Psycholinguistic approaches to therapy* (pp. 143–161). London: Whurr Publishers.

Burdette, H. L., & Whitaker, R. C. (2005). Resurrecting free play in young children: Looking beyond fitness and fatness to attention, affiliation, and affect. *Pediatric Adolescent Medicine, 159*(1), 46–50.

Burns, J. M., Andrews, G., & Szabo, M. (2002). Depression in young people: What causes it and can we prevent it? *Medical Journal of Australia, 177*(7), 93–96.

Cadima, J., Leal, T., & Burchinal, M. (2010). The quality of teacher-student interactions: Associations with first graders' academic and behavioural outcomes. *School Psychology, 48*(6), 457–482.

Campos, J. J., Frankel, C. B., & Camras, L. (2004). On the nature of emotion regulation. *Child Development, 75*(2), 377–394.

Carey, T. A., & Bourbon, W. T. (2004). Countercontrol: A new look at some old problems. *Intervention in School and Clinic, 40*(1), 3–9.

Caselman, T. (2007). *Teaching children empathy: The social emotion.* Chapin, SC: Southlight Inc.

Cassady, J. C., & Johnson, R. E. (2002). Cognitive anxiety and academic performance. *Contemporary Educational Psychology, 27*(2), 270–295.

Chorney, D. B., Detweiler, M. F., Morris, T. L., & Kuhn, B. R. (2008). The interplay of sleep disturbance, anxiety, and depression in children. *Pediatric Psychology, 33*(4), 339–348.

Clark, D. A., & Beck, A. T. (2010). *Cognitive therapy of anxiety disorders: Science and practice.* New York: Guilford Press.

Cook, K. V. (2000). You have to have somebody watching over your back, and if that's God, then that's mighty big: The church's role in the resilience of inner-city youth. *Adolescence, 35*(140), 717–731.

Coplan, R. J., Closson, L. M., & Arbeau, K. A. (2007). Gender differences in the behavioural associates of loneliness and social dissatisfaction in kindergarten. *Child Psychology and Psychiatry, 48*(10), 988–995.

Covey, S. R. (1990). *The 7 habits of highly effective people.* New York: Fireside.

Crick, N. R. (1995). Relational aggression: The role of intent attributions, feelings, and provocation type. *Development and Psychopathology, 7*(2), 313–322.

Crick, N. R., Ostrov, J. M., & Kawabata, Y. (2007). Relational aggression and gender: An overview. In D. J. Flannery, A. T. Vazsonyi, & I. D. Walman (Eds.), *Cambridge handbook of violent behaviour and aggression* (pp. 245–259). New York: Cambridge Press.

Criss, M. M., Pettit, G. S., Bates, J. E., Dodge, K. A., & Lapp, A. L. (2002). Family adversity, positive peer relationships, and children's externalizing behavior: A longitudinal perspective on risk and resilience. *Child Development, 73*(4), 1220–1237.

Davison, K. K., & Lipps Birch, L. (2001). Weight status, parent reaction, and self-concept in five-year-old girls. *Pediatrics, 107*(1), 46–53.

Davison, K. K., Markey, C. N., & Lipps Birch, L. (2003). A longitudinal examination of patterns in girls' weight concerns and body dissatisfaction from ages 5 to 9 years. *International Journal of Eating Disorders, 33*(3), 320–332.

Department of Health and Ageing. (2010). *National Mental Health Report 2010.* Canberra: Commonwealth of Australia. Retrieved from http://www.health.gov.au/mentalhealth

Dockett, S., & Perry, B. (2007). *Transitions to school: Perceptions, expectations, experiences.* Sydney: University of New South Wales.

Dodge, K. A. (1986). A social information processing model of social competence in children. In M. Perlmutter (Ed.), *Eighteenth Annual Minnesota Symposium on Child Psychology* (Vol. 18, pp. 77–125). Hillsdale, NJ: JB Erlbaum.

Dodge, K. A., & Coie, J. D. (1987). Social-information-processing factors in reactive and proactive aggression in children's peer groups. *Personality and Social Psychology, 53*(6), 1146–1158.

Doherty, W. (2000). *Take back your kids: Confident parenting in turbulent times.* Notre Dame, IN: Sorin Books.

Dreikurs Ferguson, E. (2010). Adler's innovative contributions regarding the need to belong. *Individual Psychology, 66*(1), 1–7.

Dunn, J. (1988). *The beginnings of social understanding.* Cambridge, MA: Harvard University.

Dunn, J., Brown, J., & Beardsall, L. (1991). Family talk about feeling states and children's later understanding of others' emotions. *Developmental Psychology, 27*(3), 448–455.

Dweck, C. (2006). *Mindset: The new psychology of success.* New York: Random House.

East, P. L. (2010). Children's provision of family caregiving: Benefit or burden? *Child Development Perspectives, 4*(1), 55–61.

Eckert, L. E., Miller, D. N., DuPaul, G. J., & Riley-Tillman, T. C. (2003). Adolescent suicide prevention: School psychologists' acceptability of school-based programs. *School Psychology Review, 32*(1), 57–76.

Eisen, A. R., & Engler, L. B. (2007). *Helping your socially vulnerable child.* Oakland, CA: New Harbinger.

Eisenberg, N., Spinrad, T. L., Fabes, R. A., Reiser, M., Cumberland, A., Shepard, S. A., Valiente, C., Losoya, S. H., Guthrie, I. K., & Thompson, M. (2004). The relations of effortful control and impulsivity to children's resiliency and adjustment. *Child Development, 75*(1), 25–46

Elkind, D. (2001). *The hurried child: Growing up too fast too soon.* Cambridge, MA: Perseus.

Engleberg, I. N., & Wynn, D. R. (2010). *Working in groups: Communication principles and strategies.* Boston: Allyn & Bacon.

Erikson, E. H. (1963). *Childhood and society.* New York: Norton.

Fenty, N. S., Miller, M. A., & Lampi, A. (2008). 20 ways to embed social skills instruction in inclusive settings. *Intervention in School and Clinic, 43*(3), 186–192.

Field, E. M. (2007). *Bully blocking: Six secrets to help children deal with teasing and bullying.* Sydney: Finch Publishing.

Fisher, P. H., Masia-Warner, C., & Klein, R. G. (2004). Skills for social and academic success: A school-based intervention for social anxiety disorder in adolescents. *Clinical Child and Family Psychology Review, 7*(4), 241–249.

Fombonne, E. (2005). Epidemiology of autistic disorder and other pervasive developmental disorders. *Clinical Psychiatry, 66*(10), 3–8.

Fredrickson, B. L., & Branigan, C. (2005). Positive emotions broaden the scope of attention and thought-action repertoires. *Cognition and Emotion, 19*(3), 313–332.

Fullan, M. G., & Hargreaves, A. (1996). *What's worth fighting for in our school?* New York: Teachers College Press.

Galaxy Research. (2011). *The Herald Sun Victorian Teachers Survey.* Melbourne: Author.

Gardner, H. (1993). *Frames of mind: The theory of multiple intelligences.* London: Fontana.

Garrard, J. (2009). *Active transport: Children and young people. An overview of recent evidence.* Melbourne: VicHealth.

Geake, J. G., & Cooper, P. W. (2003). Implications of cognitive neuroscience for education. *Westminster Studies in Education, 26*(10), 7–20.

Gentile, D. A., Choo, H., Liau, A., Sim, T., Li, D., Fung, D., & Khoo, A. (2011). Pathological video game use among youths: A two-year longitudinal study. *Pediatrics, 127*(2), E319–E329.

George, R. (2007). *Girls in a goldfish bowl: Moral regulation, ritual and the use of power amongst inner city girls.* Rotterdam, The Netherlands: Sense Publishers.

Gibbs, J. (2006). *Reaching all by creating tribes learning communities.* Windsor, CA: CenterSource Systems, LLC.

Gill, T. P., Baur, L. A., Bauman, A. E., Steinbeck, K. S., Storlien, L. H., Fiatarone Singh, M. A., Brand-Miller, J. C., Colagiuri, S., & Caterson, I. D. (2009). Childhood obesity in Australia remains a widespread health concern that warrants population-wide prevention programs. *Medical Journal of Australia, 190*(3), 146–148.

Ginsburg, K. R. (2007). The importance of play in promoting healthy child development and maintaining strong parent-child bonds. *Pediatrics, 119*(1), 182–191.

Goleman, D. (1996). *Emotional intelligence: Why it can matter more than IQ.* London: Bloomsbury.

Goleman, D. (1997). *Working with emotional intelligence.* London: Bloomsbury.

Graham, A. P. (1997). *Seasons for growth.* North Sydney, NSW: Mary MacKillop Foundation.

Graham, A., Phelps, R., Maddison, C., & Fitzgerald, R. (2011). Supporting children's mental health in schools: Teachers views. *Teachers and Teaching, 17*(4), 479–496.

Graziano, P. A., Reavis, R. D., Keane, S. P., & Calkins, S. D. (2007). The role of emotion regulation in children's early academic success. *School Psychology, 45*(1), 3–19.

Green, D., Oswald, M., & Spears, B. (2007). Teachers' (mis)understandings of resilience. *International Education, 8*(2), 133–144.

Grose, M. (2000). *One step ahead: Raising 3–12 year olds.* Sydney: Random House.

Guest, A., & Schneider, B. (2003). Adolescents' extracurricular participation in context: The mediating effects of schools, communities, and identity. *Sociology of Education, 76*(2), 89–109.

Hanewald, R. (2011). Reviewing the literature on 'at-risk' and resilient children and young people. *Journal of Teacher Education, 36*(2), 16–29.

Healey, J. (Ed.). (2009). *Managing stress.* Thirroul, NSW: Spinney.

Helfert, S., & Warschburger, P. (2011). A prospective study on the impact of peer and parental pressure on body dissatisfaction in adolescent girls and boys. *Body Image, 8*(2), 101–109.

Hillier, L., Jones, T., Monagle, M., Overton, N., Ghan, L., Blackman, J., & Mitchell, A. (2010). *Writing themselves in 3: The third national study on the sexual health and wellbeing of same sex attracted and gender questioning young people.* Melbourne: Australian Research Centre in Sex, Health and Society, La Trobe University.

Holder, M. D., & Coleman, B. (2008). The contribution of temperament, popularity, and physical appearance to children's happiness. *Happiness Studies, 9*(2), 279–302.

Horner, B., Downie, J., Hay, D., & Wichmann, H. (2007). Grandparent-headed families in Australia. *Family Matters, 76* (Autumn), 76–84.

Howard, S., & Johnson, B. (2000). What makes the difference? Children and teachers talk about resilient outcomes for children 'at risk'. *Educational Studies, 26*(3), 321–337.

Hromek, R. (2007). *Emotional coaching: A practical programme to support young people.* London: Paul Chapman Publishing.

Hubbard, J. A. (2001). Emotion expression processes in children's peer interaction: The role of peer rejection, aggression, and gender. *Child Development, 72*(5), 1426–1438.

Hughes, J. N., & Kwok, O. (2006). Classroom engagement mediates the effect of teacher-student support on elementary students' peer acceptance: A prospective analysis. *School Psychology, 43*(6), 465–480.

Iglowstein, I., Jenni, O. G., Molinari, L., & Largo, R. H. (2003). Sleep duration from infancy to adolescence: Reference values and generational trends. *Pediatrics, 111*(2), 302–307.

Irving, L. M. (2000). Promoting size acceptance in elementary school children: The EDAP puppet program. *Eating Disorders, 8*(3), 221–232.

Jobe-Shields, L., Cohen, R., & Parra, G. R. (2011). Patterns of change in children's loneliness. *Merrill-Palmer Quarterly, 57*(1), 25–47.

Kawabata, Y., Alink, L., Tseng, W-L., Ijzendoorn, M., & Crick, N. (2011). Maternal and paternal parenting styles associated with relational aggression in children and adolescents: A conceptual analysis and meta-analytic review. *Developmental Review, 31*(4), 240–278.

King, N. J., Ollier, K., Iacuone, R., Schuster, S., Bays, K., Gullone, E., Ollendick, T. H. (1989). Fears of children and adolescents: A cross-sectional Australian study using the revised fear survey schedule for children. *Child Psychology and Psychiatry, 30*(5), 775–784.

Klima, T., & Repetti, R. L. (2008). Children's peer relations and their psychological adjustment. differences between close friendships and the larger peer group. *Merrill-Palmer Quarterly, 54*(2), 151–178.

Klomek, A. B., Marrocco, F., Kleinman, M., Schonfeld, I. S., & Gould, M. S. (2007). Bullying, depression, and suicidality in adolescents. *American Academy of Child and Adolescent Psychiatry, 46*(1), 40–49.

Krochak, L. A., & Ryan, T. G. (2007). The challenge of identifying gifted/learning disabled students. *International Journal of Special Education, 22*(3), 44–54.

Ladd, G. W. (1999). Peer relationships and social competence during early and middle childhood. *Annual Review of Psychology, 50*(1), 333–359.

Levykh, M. G., (2008). The affective establishment and maintenance of Vygotsky's zone of proximal development. *Educational Theory, 58*(1), 83–101.

Liu, A. H., & Murphy, J. R. (2003). Hygiene hypothesis: Fact or fiction. *Allergy and Clinical Immunology, 111*(3), 471–478.

Luby, J. L. (2010). Preschool depression: The importance of identification of depression early in development. *Current Directions in Psychological Science, 19*(2), 91–95.

Ma, X. (2003). Sense of belonging to school: Can schools make a difference? *Educational Research, 96*(6), 340–349.

Maag, J. W. (2008). Rational-emotive therapy to help teachers control their emotions and behaviour when dealing with disagreeable students. *Intervention in School and Clinic, 44*(1), 52–57.

Madden, S., Morris, A., Zurynski, Y. A., Kohn, M., & Elliot, E. J. (2009). Burden of eating disorders in 5–13-year-old children in Australia. *Medical Journal of Australia, 190*(8), 410–414.

Magnuson, C. S., & Starr, M. F. (2000). How early is too early to begin life career planning? The importance of the elementary school years. *Journal of Career Development, 27*(2), 89–101.

Malatesta, C. Z., & Haviland, J. M. (1982). Learning display rules: The socialization of emotional expression in infancy. *Child Development, 53*(4), 991–1003.

Malecki, C. K., & Elliott, S. N. (2002). Children's social behaviours as predictors of academic achievement: A longitudinal analysis. *School Psychology Quarterly, 17*(1), 1–23.

Mandleco, B. L., & Craig, P. J. (2000). An organisational framework for conceptualising resilience in children. *Child and Adolescent Psychiatric Nursing, 13*(3), 99–112.

Maslow, A. (1962). *Toward a psychology of belonging.* Princeton, NJ: Van Nostrand.

Masten, A. S., & Coatsworth, J. D. (1998). The development of competence in favourable and unfavourable environments: Lessons from research on successful children. *American Psychologist, 53*(2), 205–220.

McGrath, H., & Noble, T. (2003). *Bounce back!* Sydney: Pearson Education.

Meadows, S. O., McLanahan, S. S., & Brooks-Gunn, J. (2007). Parental depression and anxiety and early childhood behavior problems across family types. *Marriage and Family, 69*(5), 1162–1177.

Mehrabian, A. (1981). *Silent messages: Implicit communication of emotions and attitudes.* Belmont, CA: Wadsworth.

Minnard, C. (2002). A strong building: Foundation of protective factors in schools. *Children and Schools, 24*(4), 233–246.

Miyakawa, J. (2001). Performance on the matching familiar figures test: Classroom behaviors, and school achievements of elementary school children in Japan. *Japanese Journal of Psychology, 72*(5), 435–442.

Mori, I., & Nairn, A. (2011). *Children's wellbeing in UK, Sweden and Spain: The role of inequality and materialism. A qualitative study.* London: UNICEF. Retrieved from http://www.unicef.org.uk/childwellbeing

Morrison, B. (2002). Bullying and victimisation in schools: A restorative justice approach. *Trends and Issues in Crime and Criminal Justice, 219,* 1–6. Canberra: Australian Institute of Criminology.

Murray, B., & Fortinberry, A. (2006). *Raising an optimistic child: A proven plan for depression-proofing young children – for life.* New York: McGraw-Hill.

Neil, A. L., & Christensen, H. (2007). Australian school-based prevention and early intervention programs for anxiety and depression: A systematic review. *Medical Journal of Australia, 186*(6), 305–308.

Nesdale, D., & Duffy, A. (2011). Social identity, peer group rejection, and young children's reactive, displaced, and proactive aggression. *Developmental Psychology, 29*(4), 823–841.

Newberry, M., & Davis, H. A. (2008). The role of elementary teachers' conceptions of closeness to students on their differential behaviour in the classroom. *Teaching and Teacher Education, 24*(8), 1965–1985.

Nickolite, A., & Doll, B. (2008). Resilience applied in school: Strengthening classroom environments for learning. *Canadian Journal of School Psychology, 23*(1), 94–113.

Olds, T. S., Tomkinson, G. R., Ferrar, K. E., & Maher, C. A. (2010). Trends in the prevalence of childhood overweight and obesity in Australia between 1985 and 2008. *International Journal of Obesity, 34*(1), 57–66.

Olweus, D. (1978). *Aggression in the schools: Bullies and whipping boys.* Washington, DC: Hemisphere.

Olweus, D. (1993). *Bullying at school: What we know and what we can do.* Oxford: Blackwell.

O'Rourke, J., & Cooper, M. (2010). Lucky to be happy: A study of happiness in Australian primary students. *Educational & Developmental Psychology, 10,* 94–107.

O'Sullivan, K. R., & Russell, H. (2006). Parents and professionals: Breaking cycles of blame. *Reclaiming Children and Youth, 15*(1), 37–39.

Oswald, M., Johnson, B., & Howard, S. (2003). Quantifying and evaluating resilience-promoting factors: Teachers' beliefs and perceived roles. *Research in Education, 70,* 50–64.

Panju, M. (2008). *7 Successful strategies to promote emotional intelligence in the classroom.* London: Network Continuum.

Paquette, M. C., & Raine, K. (2004). Sociocultural context of women's body image. *Social Science & Medicine, 59*(5), 1047–1058.

Parkinson, P., & Kazzi, A. (2011). *For kids' sake: Repairing the social environment for Australian children and young people.* Sydney: Vos Foundation/University of Sydney.

Passy, J. (2010). *Cued articulation: Consonants and vowels* (Rev. ed.). Melbourne: ACER Press.

Patall, E. A., Cooper, H., & Wynn, S. R. (2010). The effectiveness and relative importance of choice in the classroom. *Educational Psychology, 102*(4), 896–915.

Pellegrini, A. D. (2009). Research and policy on children's play. *Child Development Perspectives, 3*(2), 131–136.

Perrin, E. C. (2002). Technical report: Co-parent or second-parent adoption by same-sex parents. *Pediatrics, 109*(2), 341–344.

Peters Mayer, D. (2008). *Overcoming school anxiety: How to help your child deal with separation, tests, homework, bullies, math phobia, and other worries.* New York: AMACON.

Phillips, D. (1984). The illusion of incompetence among academically competent children. *Child Development, 55,* 2000–2016.

Pincus, D. B., & Friedman, A. G. (2004). Improving children's coping with everyday stress: Transporting treatment interventions to the school setting. *Clinical Child and Family Psychology Review, 7*(4), 223–240.

Proctor, J. (2005). Integrating career education in a primary school. *Australian Journal of Career Development, 14*(3), 13–17.

Puhl, R. M., & Latner, J. D. (2007). Stigma, obesity, and the health of the nation's children. *Psychological Bulletin, 133*(4), 557–580.

Rae, T. (2006). *Good choices: Teaching young people aged 8 to 11 to make positive decisions about their own lives.* London: Paul Chapman Publishing.

Rapee, R. M. (1998). *Overcoming shyness and social phobia.* Northvale, NJ: Jason Aronson.

Raver, C. C. (2004). Placing emotional self-regulation in sociocultural and socioeconomic contexts. *Child Development, 75*(2), 346–353.

Regneruis, M. D., & Elder, G. H. (2003). Religion and vulnerability among low-risk adolescents. *Social Science Research, 32*(4), 633–658.

Reynhout, G., & Carter, M. (2006). Social stories for children with disabilities. *Journal of Autism and Developmental Disorders, 36*(4), 445–469.

Riley, D., Juan, R.S., Klinder, J., & Ramminger, A. (2008). *Social and emotional development: Connecting science and practice in early childhood settings.* St. Paul, MN: Redleaf Press.

Rivers, I., Poteat, V. P., Noret, N., & Ashurst, N. (2009). Observing bullying at school: The mental health implications of witness status. *School Psychology Quarterly, 24*(4), 211–223.

Roffey, S. (2008). Emotional literacy and the ecology of school wellbeing. *Education and Child Psychology, 25*(2), 29–39.

Rosen, D. S. (2010). Identification and management of eating disorders in children and adolescents. *Paediatrics, 126*(6), 1240–1253.

Rosner, R., Kruse, J., & Hagl, M. (2010). A meta-analysis of interventions for bereaved children and adolescents. *Death Studies, 34*(2), 99–136.

Rowe, K. J. (2003). The importance of teacher quality as a key determinant of students' experiences and outcomes of schooling. Melbourne: Australian Council for Educational Research. Retrieved from http:.//www.research.acer.edu.au/research_ conference_2003/3

Rowe, K. J., & Rowe, K. S. (2000). *Inquiry into the education of boys: Submission to the House of Representatives Standing Committee on Employment, Education and Workplace Relations.* Melbourne: Australian Council for Educational Research and the Department of General Paediatrics, Royal Children's Hospital. Retrieved from http://www.aph.gov.au/house/committee/edt/Eofb/index.htm

Rubin, K. H., Bukowski, W., & Parker, J. (2006). Peer interactions, relationships, and groups. In N. Eisenberg (Ed.), *Handbook of child psychology: Social, emotional, and personality development.* (pp. 571–645). New York: Wiley.

Rubin, K. H., Coplan, R. J., & Bowker, J. C. (2009). Social withdrawal in childhood. *Annual Review of Psychology, 60,* 141–171.

Russo, R., & Boman, P. (2007). Primary school teachers' ability to recognise resilience in their students. *Australian Educational Researcher, 34*(1), 17–32.

Rydell, A., Berlin, L., & Bohlin, G. (2003). Emotionality, emotion regulation, and adaptation among 5-to-8-year-old children. *Emotion, 3*(1), 30–47.

Schutz, P. A., & DeCuir, J. T. (2002). Inquiry on emotions in education. *Educational Psychologist, 37*(2), 125–134.

Seligman, M. (2000). Positive psychology. *American Psychologist, 55*(1), 5–14.

Seligman, M. (2007). *The optimistic child: A proven program to safeguard children against depression and build lifelong resilience.* New York: Houghton-Mifflin.

Seligman, M. (2008, August 8). Positive education and the new prosperity: Australia's edge. *Education Today,* pp. 20–21. Retrieved from http://www.minniscomms.com.au/educationtoday/article/Positive-education-and-the-new-prosperity-546

Shoda, Y., Mischel, W., & Peake, P. K. (1990). Predicting adolescent cognitive and self-regulatory competencies from preschool delay of gratification: Identifying diagnostic conditions. *Developmental Psychology, 26*(6), 978–986.

Siccone, F., & Canfield, J. (1993). *101 ways to develop student self-esteem and responsibility, Volume II: The power to succeed in school and beyond.* Boston: Allyn & Bacon.

Simmons, R. (2002). *Odd girl out: The hidden culture of aggression in girls.* Melbourne: Schwartz Publishing.

Skinner, B. F. (1953). *Science and human behaviour.* New York: Free Press.

Spence, S., Burns, J., Boucher, S., Glover, S., Graetz, B., Kay, D., Patton, G. C., & Sawer, M. G. (2005). The beyondblue schools research initiative: Conceptual framework and intervention. *Australasian Psychiatry, 13*(2), 159–164.

Stanley, R. M., Ridley, K., & Olds, T. S. (2011). The type and prevalence of activities performed by Australian children during the lunchtime and after school periods. *Science and Medicine in Sport, 14*(3), 227–232.

Stein, N. (1999). *Classrooms and courtrooms: Facing sexual harassment in K-12 schools.* New York: Teachers College Press.

Stewart, E. B. (2008). School structural characteristics, student effort, peer associations, and parental involvement. *Education and Urban Society, 40*(2), 179–204.

Stormont, M. A. (2008). Increase academic success for children with ADHD using sticky notes and highlighters. *Intervention in School and Clinic: 43*(5), 305–308.

Strauss, R. S., & Pollack, H. A. (2003). Social marginalization of overweight children. *Pediatrics and Adolescent Medicine, 157*(8), 746–752.

Suckling, A., & Temple, C. (2008). *Cool calm kids.* Melbourne: ACER Press.

Sutterby, J. A. (2009). What kids don't get to do anymore and why. *Childhood Education, 8*(5), 289–292.

Troop-Gordon, W., & Quenette, A. (2010). Children's perceptions of their teacher's responses to students' peer harassment. *Merrill-Palmer Quarterly, 56*(3), 333–360.

Tucci, J., Mitchell, J., & Goddard, C. (2007). *Modern children in Australia*. Melbourne: Australian Childhood Foundation.

Valkenburg, P. M., & Peter, J. (2009). Social consequences of the internet for adolescents. *Current Directions in Psychological Science, 18*(1), 1–5.

VicHealth. (2011). *Towards active and independently mobile children. Survey review*. Melbourne: Victorian Health Promotion Foundation.

Vierhaus, M., & Lohaus, A. (2009). Children's perception of relations between anger or anxiety and coping: Continuity and discontinuity of relational structures. *Social Development, 18*(3), 747–763.

Vygotsky, L. S. (1978). *Mind in society: The development of higher mental process*. Cambridge, MA: Harvard University.

Walker, L. J., Hennig, K. H., & Krettenauer, T. (2000). Parent and peer contexts for children's moral reasoning development. *Child Development, 71*(4), 1033–1048.

Wang, J., Nansel, T. R., & Iannotti, R. J. (2011). Cyber and traditional bullying: Differential association with depression. *Adolescent Health, 48*(4), 415–417.

Watson, R. (2010). *Future minds: How the digital age is changing our minds, why this matters, and what we can do about it*. London: Nicholas Brealey.

Webster-Stratton, C. (2002). *How to promote children's social and emotional competence*. London: Paul Chapman Publishing.

Weissbourd, R. (2009). *The parents we mean to be. How well-intentioned adults undermine children's moral and emotional development*. Boston: Houghton Mifflin.

Weissbourd, R. (2011, April 11). Morality, happiness and self-esteem. *The New York Times*. Retrieved from http://parenting.blogs.nytimes.com/2011/04/11/teaching-children-to-do-good/

Whitted, K. S. (2011). Understanding how social and emotional skill deficits contribute to school failure. *Preventing School Failure, 55*(1), 10–16.

Williams, Z. (2006). *The commercialisation of children*. London: Compass.

Wilson, B. J. (2008). Media and children's aggression, fear and altruism. *The Future of Children, 18*(1), 87–118.

Woolfolk, A., & Margetts, K. (2010). *Educational psychology*. Frenchs Forest, NSW: Pearson.

Wray, J., & Williams, K. (2007). *The prevalence of autism in Australia: Can it be established from existing data?* Report commissioned by the Advisory Board on Autism Spectrum Disorders.

Yoon, J. S., & Kerber, K. (2003). Bullying: Elementary teachers' attitudes and intervention strategies. *Research in Education, 69*, 27–35.

Zeman, J., & Garber, J. (1996). Display rules for anger, sadness and pain: It depends on who is watching. *Child Development, 67*(3), 957–973.

Zeman, J., & Shipman, K. (1996). Children's expression of negative affect: Reasons and methods. *Developmental Psychology, 32*(5), 842–849.

Zimmerman, B. J. (2000). Attaining self-regulation: A social cognitive perspective. In M. Boekarts, P. Pintrich & M. Zeidner (Eds.), *Self-regulations: Theory, research, and application* (pp. 13–39). Orlando, FL: Academic.

Zins, J. E., Weissberg, R. P., Wang, M. C., & Walberg, H. J. (2004). *Building academic success on social and emotional learning.* New York: Teachers College Press.

Zirpoli, T. J. (2010). *Behavior management: Positive applications for teachers.* Saddle River, NJ: Pearson Education.

Zubrick, S. R., Wood, L., Villanueva, K., Wood, G., Giles-Corti, B., & Christian, H. (2010). *Nothing but fear itself: Parental fear as a determinant of child physical activity and independent mobility,* Melbourne: VicHealth.

Index

What Teachers Need to Know About series

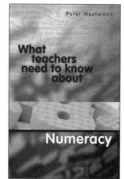

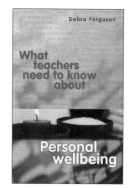

sales@acer.edu.au | 03 9277 5447 | Order online: http://shop.acer.edu.au

www.acer.edu.au/publications/education